Delights and Warnings

In this anthology John and Gillian Beer have chosen poems to appeal to children and reflect their interests.

Some of the poems tell a story, an adventure or an anecdote. There are poems about heroes and heroines, and poems that express sympathy with the underdog. Some poems look at the world of nature, at people, animals and plants. Other poems send shivers up and down the spine, and are full of mystery, spells and strangeness.

There are traditional poems and modern poems, short poems and long poems, funny poems and sad poems.

The eye-catching illustrations by Giovanni Caselli often help to explain a difficult idea or give life to a scene from the past.

JOHN and GILLIAN BEER both lecture in English at Cambridge University, and have written several books about English poets. They have three young children.

GIOVANNI CASELLI comes from Florence in Italy, although he has worked in England for the past eight years. He is married with two children and lives in Brighton.

A MACDONALD BOOK

© Macdonald Educational Ltd 1979

First published in Great Britain in 1979

Reprinted 1982

Paperback edition 1984

Reprinted 1986

All rights reserved

ISBN 0 356 11212 8

Printed and bound in Great Britain by
Purnell Book Production Ltd
Paulton, Bristol

Members of BPCC plc

Published by Macdonald & Co (Publishers) Ltd
Maxwell House
74 Worship Street
London, EC2A 2EN

Delights and Warnings

a new anthology of poems
selected by
John and Gillian Beer
illustrated by
Giovanni Caselli

Macdonald

Contents

HEROES AND VICTIMS

MAGIC AND MYSTERY

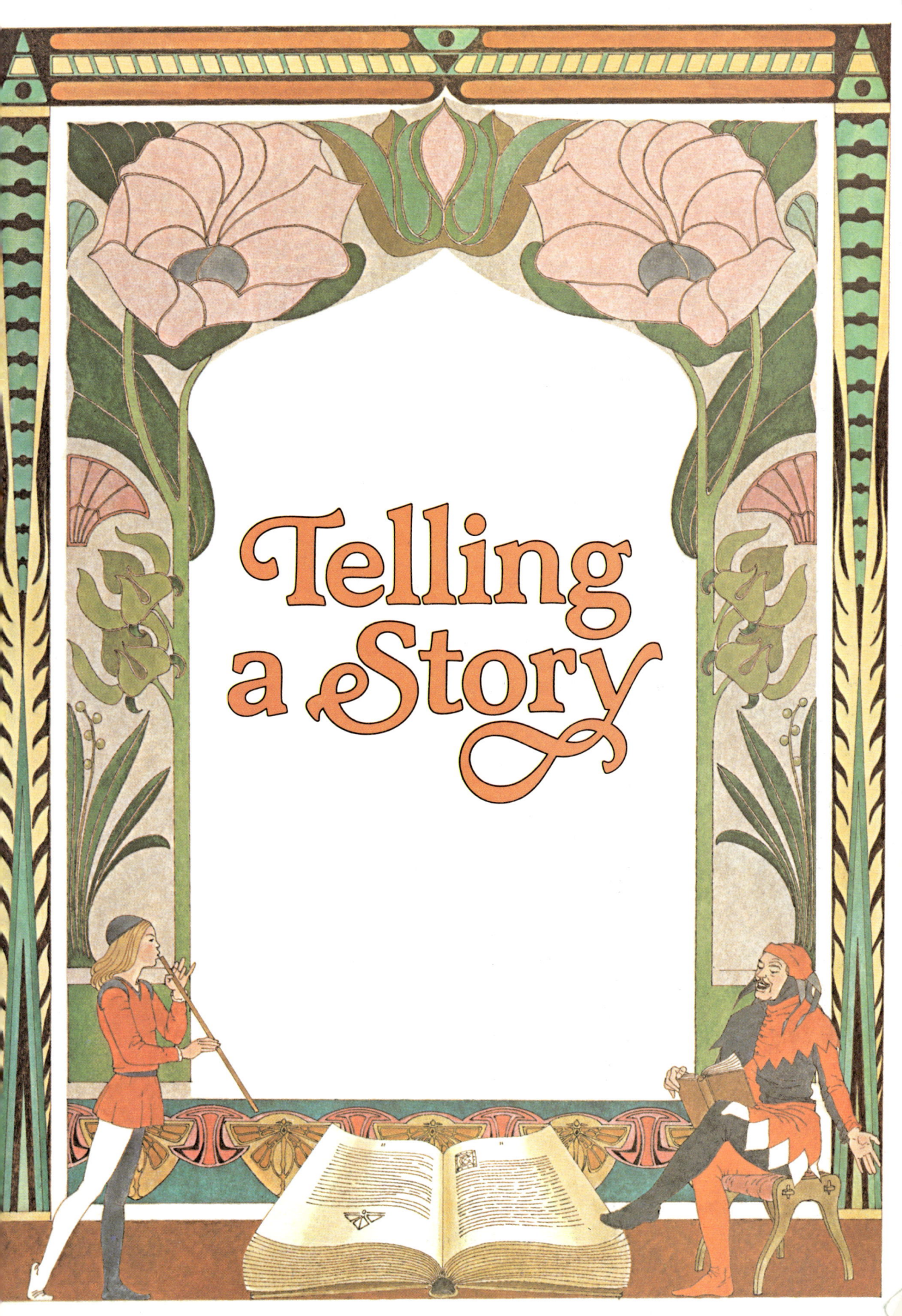

Telling a Story

About the poems

We all spend much of our lives telling stories. We go home and tell each other what has happened to us during the day, saving up especially the things that are surprising, frightening or important to us in some way.

The man in the first poem isn't just telling us about bits and pieces of his childhood; he is explaining through this story why he had difficulty in getting on with people when he was older. At the same time he is pointing out how we are very often attracted by things that frighten us.

The small boy in **The Pond** feels this attraction (he is a West Indian—can you see which word tells us that?). He plucks up his courage to face the terrifying pond, only to find that the terror the pond holds is nothing more than a reflection of his own fears.

This idea is carried on in **maggie and milly and molly and may**, who, on a visit to the beach, all find things which reflect themselves in some way.

Many of the poems in this section are about the sea, because that is where some of the best stories happen. The sea is beautiful and exciting, but it can also be dangerous, as we discover in **The Sands of Dee**. Here the description of the sea— it is 'cruel' and 'hungry'—reflects the emotions of the story-teller, just as nature reflected the feelings of the small boy in **The Pond**.

Clarence's Dream is also about death by drowning. In Shakespeare's play *Richard III*, from which it is taken, the speech makes us suspect that something cruel is going to happen to Clarence at the hands of Gloucester—and it does. (So, here is a story which makes us guess at another, worse, story.) It is a vivid description of a nightmare in which everything is dead yet seems almost normal. The choking feeling described at the end is the one we often experience in nightmares.

In all these poems the poet's emotion comes across very strongly. But in some older poems telling a story (often called ballads, because they were meant to be sung rather than simply read aloud), the feeling is not at first so easy to find.

In **Sir Patrick Spens** we are told the story of a shipwreck, with each of the characters speaking as if it were a play. Notice how the poet then turns away from the speeches of the characters to look at the scene from a distance, and to think about the people waiting on the land. How would you film this story? Does the poem give you any ideas for scenes?

The next two poems (**Six Dukes Went a-Fishing** and **The Duke of Grafton**) show us how the same story can come out quite differently when told by different people. Even the name of the drowned man is not the same! Do you find that each of these poems is better than the other in some ways? Or is one better in every way?

Since the time of ballad writers, poets have worked out lots of different ways to tell stories. The poem **Stupidity Street** is written very simply, but it is as full of emotion and anger as the apparently more straightforward **Gresford Disaster.** This is a modern ballad, and although it resembles **Sir Patrick Spens** in some ways, it differs both in being more angry about the actions that led to the disaster, and in finding someone to blame for it.

In the poem **Snake** there is blame too, but the poet blames himself, not someone else. Do you think he is right? Does he want to make us feel what the snake felt? If so, how does he do it?

Snake is a straightforward story with a beginning, a middle and an end, but what about **Ozymandias**? Nothing happens, except that one man describes something he has seen to another. Where is the story in this poem then?

So far we have been looking at serious poems. The rest of the poems in this section are funnier—the sort of stories people tell you to make you laugh. When a poet is telling a serious story, he will often use the shape of his lines to make an important sentence stand out (as the last line in **Ozymandias** stands out just because it *is* the last line).

The comic poet uses the shape of his poem to help with the fun: notice, for example, how the cramming of the words into the lines of **The Rest of the Day is Your Own** makes the poem sound busy. Try reading it aloud, and see if you don't begin to feel tired! The poet sometimes likes to have a twist in the last line, too. Is there one here?

There's nothing particularly surprising in the last line of **The Flight of the Rollercoaster;** but there is a surprise in the poem as a whole—where does it begin? Like **Mad Ad** it tells a fantastic story, but is it the same kind of poem? One poem takes off and does not really end, while the other ends with a punch-line. Does that make any difference? Which other poem in this section do you think is most like **Mad Ad**? Have a look at **Surprise! or the Escapologist**. It sounds rather like **Mad Ad**, but at the end we can go on imagining the story, as we can in **The Flight of the Rollercoaster**.

Using your imagination is part of the fun of listening to stories. Try and imagine what the characters in **The Jumblies** and **Jabberwocky** look like. The artist has drawn what he thinks they look like, but you may find that to you they look quite different.

Jabberwocky shows, too, how you do not need to understand all the words in a poem to know what is going on. Lewis Carroll, who wrote the poem, did explain some of the words, however. You can read about them in his book, *Through the Looking Glass*.

We come back to earth with **Albert and the Lion**, which is much more the kind of story we hear people telling each other every day—though not everyone's visit to the zoo is as unlucky as this one!

The last poem of all is a rather strange story, because the real story happens just after the poem stops. But we are all so good at seeing stories in things that we don't always have to be told what the story is: we enjoy imagining it for ourselves.

'MY PARENTS KEPT ME FROM
CHILDREN WHO WERE ROUGH'

My parents kept me from children who were rough
And who threw words like stones and who wore torn clothes.
Their thighs showed through rags. They ran in the street
And climbed cliffs and stripped by the country streams.
I feared more than tigers their muscles like iron
And their jerking hands and their knees tight on my arms.
I feared the salt coarse pointing of those boys
Who copied my lisp behind me on the road.

They were lithe, they sprang out behind hedges
Like dogs to bark at our world. They threw mud
And I looked another way, pretending to smile.
I longed to forgive them, yet they never smiled.

STEPHEN SPENDER

12

SKATING

And in the frosty season, when the sun
Was set, and visible for many a mile
The cottage windows through the twilight blazed,
I heeded not the summons: clear and loud
The village clock tolled six; I wheeled about,
Proud and exulting, like an untired horse,
That cares not for its home.—All shod with steel,
We hissed along the polished ice, in games
Confederate, imitative of the chase
And woodland pleasures, the resounding horn,
The Pack loud bellowing, and the hunted hare.

So through the darkness and the cold we flew,
And not a voice was idle; with the din,
Meanwhile, the precipices rang aloud,
The leafless trees, and every icy crag
Tinkled like iron, while the distant hills
Into the tumult sent an alien sound
Of melancholy, not unnoticed, while the stars,
Eastward, were sparkling clear, and in the west
The orange sky of evening died away.

WILLIAM WORDSWORTH

THE POND

There was this pond in the village
and little boys, he heard till he was sick,
were not allowed too near.
Unfathomable pool, they said,
that swallowed men and animals just so;
and in its depths, old people said,
swam galliwasps and nameless horrors;
bright boys kept away.

Though drawn so hard by prohibitions,
the small boy, fixed in fear, kept off;
till one wet summer, grass growing lush,
paths muddy, slippery, he found himself
there, at the fabled edge.

The brooding pond was dark.
Sudden, escaping cloud, the sun
came bright; and, shimmering in guilt,
he saw his own face peering from the pool.

MERVYN MORRIS

MAGGIE AND MILLY
AND MOLLY AND MAY

maggie and milly and molly and may
went down to the beach (to play one day)

and maggie discovered a shell that sang
so sweetly she couldn't remember her troubles, and

milly befriended a stranded star
whose rays five languid fingers were;

and molly was chased by a horrible thing
which raced sideways while blowing bubbles: and

may came home with a smooth round stone
as small as a world and as large as alone.

For whatever we lose (like a you or a me)
it's always ourselves we find in the sea

E. E. CUMMINGS

THE SANDS OF DEE

'O Mary, go and call the cattle home,
    And call the cattle home,
    And call the cattle home
  Across the sands of Dee;'
The western wind was wild and dank with foam,
  And all alone went she.

The western tide crept up along the sand,
    And o'er and o'er the sand,
    And round and round the sand,
  As far as eye could see.
The rolling mist came down and hid the land:
  And never home came she.

'Oh! is it weed, or fish, or floating hair—
    A tress of golden hair,
    A drowned maiden's hair
  Above the nets at sea?
Was never salmon yet that shone so fair
  Among the stakes on Dee.'

They rowed her in across the rolling foam,
    The cruel crawling foam,
    The cruel hungry foam,
  To her grave beside the sea:
But still the boatmen hear her call the cattle home
  Across the sands of Dee.

CHARLES KINGSLEY

CLARENCE'S DREAM

Brackenbury:
What was your dream? I long to hear you tell it.
Clarence:
I thought that I had broken from the Tower,
And was embarked to cross to Burgundy;
And, in my company, my brother Gloucester;
Who from my cabin tempted me to walk
Upon the hatches: thence we looked toward
    England,
And cited up a thousand fearful times,
During the war of York and Lancaster,
That had befallen us. As we paced along
Upon the giddy footing of the hatches,
I thought that Gloucester stumbled; and,
    in falling,
Struck me, that thought to stay him, overboard,
Into the tumbling billows of the main.
Lord, Lord! I thought, what pain it was
    to drown!
What dreadful noise of waters in my ears!
What ugly sights of death within my eyes!
I thought I saw a thousand fearful wrecks;
Ten thousand men that fishes gnawed upon;
Wedges of gold, great anchors, heaps of pearl,
Inestimable stones, unvalued jewels,
All scattered in the bottom of the sea:
Some lay in dead men's skulls; and in those holes
Where eyes did once inhabit, there were crept,
As 'twere in scorn of eyes, reflecting gems,
Which woo'd the slimy bottom of the deep,
And mock'd the dead bones that lay scattered by.
Brackenbury:
Had you such leisure in the time of death
To gaze upon the secrets of the deep?
Clarence:
I thought I had; and often did I strive
To yield the ghost: but still the envious flood
Kept in my soul, and would not let it forth
To seek the empty, vast, and wandering air;
But smothered it within my panting bulk,
Which almost burst to belch it in the sea.

WILLIAM SHAKESPEARE
Richard III

17

SIR PATRICK SPENS

The King sits in Dumfermline town
    Drinking the blood-red wine:
'O, where will I get a skilly skipper
    To sail this new ship of mine?'

Then up and spoke an elder knight
    Sat at the King's right knee:
'Sir Patrick Spens is the best sailor
    That ever sailed the sea.'

The King has written a broad letter
    And sealed it with his hand,
And sent it to Sir Patrick Spens
    Was walking on the strand.

The first word that Sir Patrick read
    So loud, loud laughed he;
The next word that Sir Patrick read
    The tear blinded his eye.

'O who is the man has done this deed
    And told the King of me,
To send us out at this time of year
    To sail upon the sea?

'Be it wind, be it wet, be it hail, be it sleet,
    Our ship must sail the foam;
The king's daughter in Norway,
    'Tis I must fetch her home.'

They have mounted sail on a Monday morn
    With all the haste they may;
They have landed in Norway
    Upon a Wednesday.

———————————————

'Make haste, make haste, my merry men all,
    We sail for home at morn.'
'But how can we sail, my master dear,
    I fear a deadly storm.

They fetched a web of the silken cloth,
   Another of the twine.
They wrapped them round the good ship's side,
   And still the sea came in.

Loth, loth, were our Scottish lords
   To wet their cork-heeled shoes,
But yet ere all the play was played
   Their hats were wetted too.

O long, long may their ladies sit
   With their fans held in their hand,
Before they see Sir Patrick Spens
   Come sailing to the strand.

O long, long may the ladies stand
   With their gold combs in their hair,
All waiting for their own dear loves:
   For them they'll see no more.

There was Saturday and Sabbath-day,
   And Monday at morn,
Then featherbeds and silken sheets
   Came floating to Kinghorn.

Half o'er, half o'er to Aberdour
   'Tis fifty fathoms deep.
And there lies good Sir Patrick Spens
   With the Scots lords at his feet.

'I saw the new moon yester e'en
   With the old moon in her arm.
And if we go to sea, master,
   I fear we'll come to harm.'

They had not sailed a league, a league,
   A league but barely three,
Came wind and wet and snow and sleet
   And gurly grew the sea.

'O where will I get a pretty boy
   Will take my helm in hand,
Till I get up to the tall topmast
   To see if I can spy land?'

He had not gone a step, a step,
   A step but barely one,
When a bolt flew out of the good ship's side,
   And the salt sea it came in.

'Come back, come back, my pretty boy,
   Lest you should come to harm,
For the salt sea's in at our coat neck,
   And out at the left arm.'

SIX DUKES WENT A-FISHING

Six dukes went a-fishing
Down by the seaside.
One of them saw a dead body
Washed up by the tide.

The one spoke to the other,
These words I heard him say:
'It's the Royal Duke of Grantham
That the tide has washed away.'

They took him up to Portsmouth,
To a place where he was known;
From there up to London,
To the place where he was born.

They laid out his body
And stretched out his feet;
They covered him with flowers,
With roses so sweet.

Six dukes stood in front,
Twelve raised him from the ground,
Nine lords followed after him
Through the weeping town.

Black were their long coats,
Their walking sticks were white,
And each carried in his hand
A yellow burning light.

They laid him between two towers,
They laid him in cold clay;
And the Royal Queen of Grantham
Went weeping away.

THE DUKE OF GRAFTON

As two men were a-walking, down by the seaside
O the brave Duke of Grafton they straightway
    espied,
Said the one to the other, and thus did they say,
It is the brave Duke of Grafton that is now
    cast away.

They brought him to Portsmouth, his fame to
    make known,
And from thence to fair London, so near to
    the Crown,
They pulled out his bowels, and they stretched
    forth his feet,
They embalmed his body with spices so sweet.

All things were made ready, his funeral for to be,
Where the royal Queen Mary came there for to see,
Six lords went before him, six bore him from
    the ground,
Six Dukes walked before him in black velvet gowns.

So black was their mourning, so white were their bands!
So yellow were the flaming torches they carried in
    their hands!
The drums they did rattle, the trumpets sweetly
    sound,
While the muskets and cannons did thunder
    all around.

In Westminster Abbey 'tis now called by name,
There the great Duke of Grafton does lie in
    great fame;
In Westminster Abbey he lies in cold clay
Where the royal Queen Mary went weeping away.

STUPIDITY STREET

I saw with open eyes
Singing birds sweet
Sold in the shops
For the people to eat,
Sold in the shops of
Stupidity Street.

I saw in vision
The worm in the wheat,
And in the shops nothing
For people to eat;
Nothing for sale in
Stupidity Street.

RALPH HODGSON

THE GRESFORD DISASTER

You've heard of the Gresford disaster,
The terrible price that was paid;
Two hundred and forty-two colliers were lost
And three men of the rescue brigade.

It occurred in the month of September,
At three in the morning that pit
Was racked by a violent explosion
In the Dennis where dust lay so thick.

The gas in the Dennis deep section
Was packed like snow in a drift,
And many a man had to leave the coal-face
Before he had worked out his shift.

A fortnight before the explosion
To the shot-firer Tomlinson cried:
'If you fire that shot we'll be all blown to hell.'
And no one can say that he lied.

The fireman's reports they are missing,
The records of forty-two days,
The colliery manager had them destroyed
To cover his criminal ways.

Down there in the dark they are lying,
They died for nine shillings a day;
They've worked out their shift and it's now they
    must lie
In the darkness until judgement day.

The Lord Mayor of London's collecting
To help both the children and wives;
The owners have sent some white lilies
To pay for the colliers' lives.

Farewell our dear wives and our children,
Farewell our dear comrades as well,
Don't send your sons in the dark dreary mine,
They'll be damned like the sinners in hell.

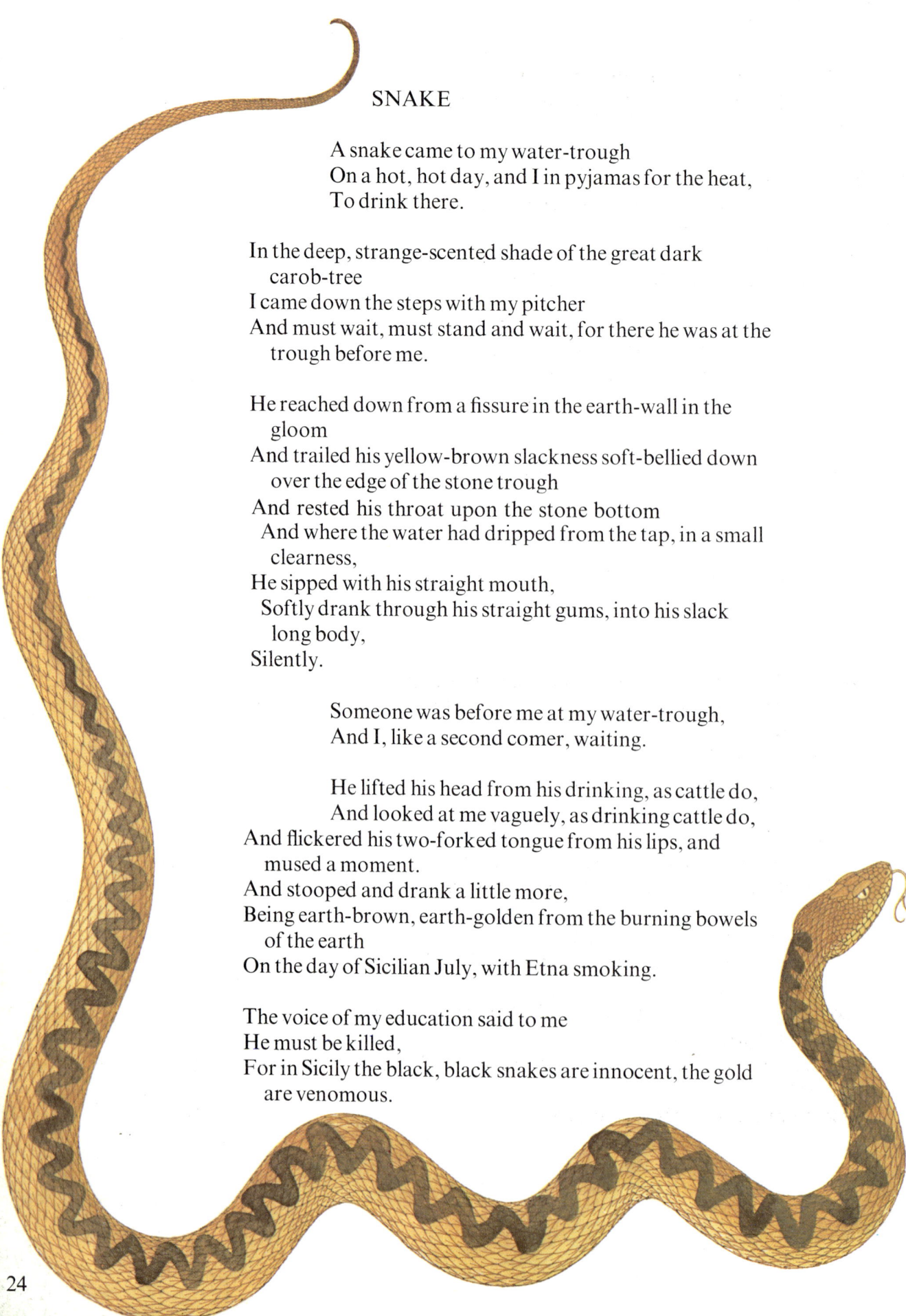

SNAKE

A snake came to my water-trough
On a hot, hot day, and I in pyjamas for the heat,
To drink there.

In the deep, strange-scented shade of the great dark
     carob-tree
I came down the steps with my pitcher
And must wait, must stand and wait, for there he was at the
     trough before me.

He reached down from a fissure in the earth-wall in the
     gloom
And trailed his yellow-brown slackness soft-bellied down
     over the edge of the stone trough
And rested his throat upon the stone bottom
   And where the water had dripped from the tap, in a small
     clearness,
He sipped with his straight mouth,
   Softly drank through his straight gums, into his slack
     long body,
Silently.

          Someone was before me at my water-trough,
          And I, like a second comer, waiting.

          He lifted his head from his drinking, as cattle do,
          And looked at me vaguely, as drinking cattle do,
And flickered his two-forked tongue from his lips, and
     mused a moment.
And stooped and drank a little more,
Being earth-brown, earth-golden from the burning bowels
     of the earth
On the day of Sicilian July, with Etna smoking.

The voice of my education said to me
He must be killed,
For in Sicily the black, black snakes are innocent, the gold
     are venomous.

24

And voices in me said, If you were a man
You would take a stick and break him now, and finish
him off.

But must I confess how I liked him,
How glad I was he had come like a guest in quiet, to drink
at my water-trough
And depart peaceful, pacified, and thankless,
Into the burning bowels of this earth?

Was it cowardice, that I dared not kill him?
Was it perversity, that I longed to talk to him?
Was it humility, to feel so honoured?
I felt so honoured.

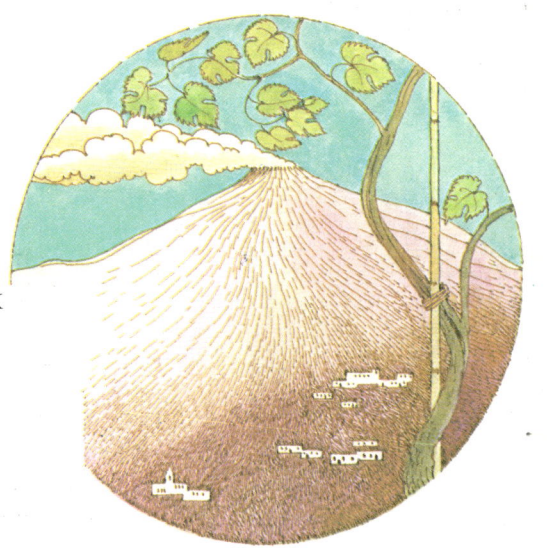

And yet those voices:
If you were not afraid, you would kill him!

And truly I was afraid, I was most afraid,
But even so, honoured still more
That he should seek my hospitality
From out the dark door of the secret earth.

He drank enough
And lifted his head, dreamily, as one who has drunken,
And flickered his tongue like a forked night on the air,
so black;
Seeming to lick his lips,
And looked around like a god, unseeing, into the air,
And slowly turned his head.
And slowly, very slowly, as if thrice adream,
Proceeded to draw his slow length curving round
And climb again the broken bank of my wall-face.

And as he put his head into that dreadful hole,
And as he slowly drew up, snake-easing his shoulders, and
entered farther,
A sort of horror, a sort of protest against his withdrawing
into that horrid black hole,
Deliberately going into the blackness, and slowly drawing
himself after,
Overcame me now his back was turned.

I looked round, I put down my pitcher,
I picked up a clumsy log
And threw it at the water-trough with a clatter.

I think it did not hit him,
But suddenly that part of him that was left behind convulsed
    in undignified haste,
Writhed like lightning, and was gone
Into the black hole, the earth-lipped fissure in the wall-front,
At which, in the intense still noon, I stared with fascination.

And immediately I regretted it.
I thought how paltry, how vulgar, what a mean act!
I despised myself and the voices of my accursed human
    education.

And I thought of the albatross,
And I wished he would come back, my snake.

For he seemed to me again like a king.
Like a king in exile, uncrowned in the underworld,
Now due to be crowned again.

And so, I missed my chance with one of the lords
Of life.
And I have something to expiate;
A pettiness.

D. H. LAWRENCE

26

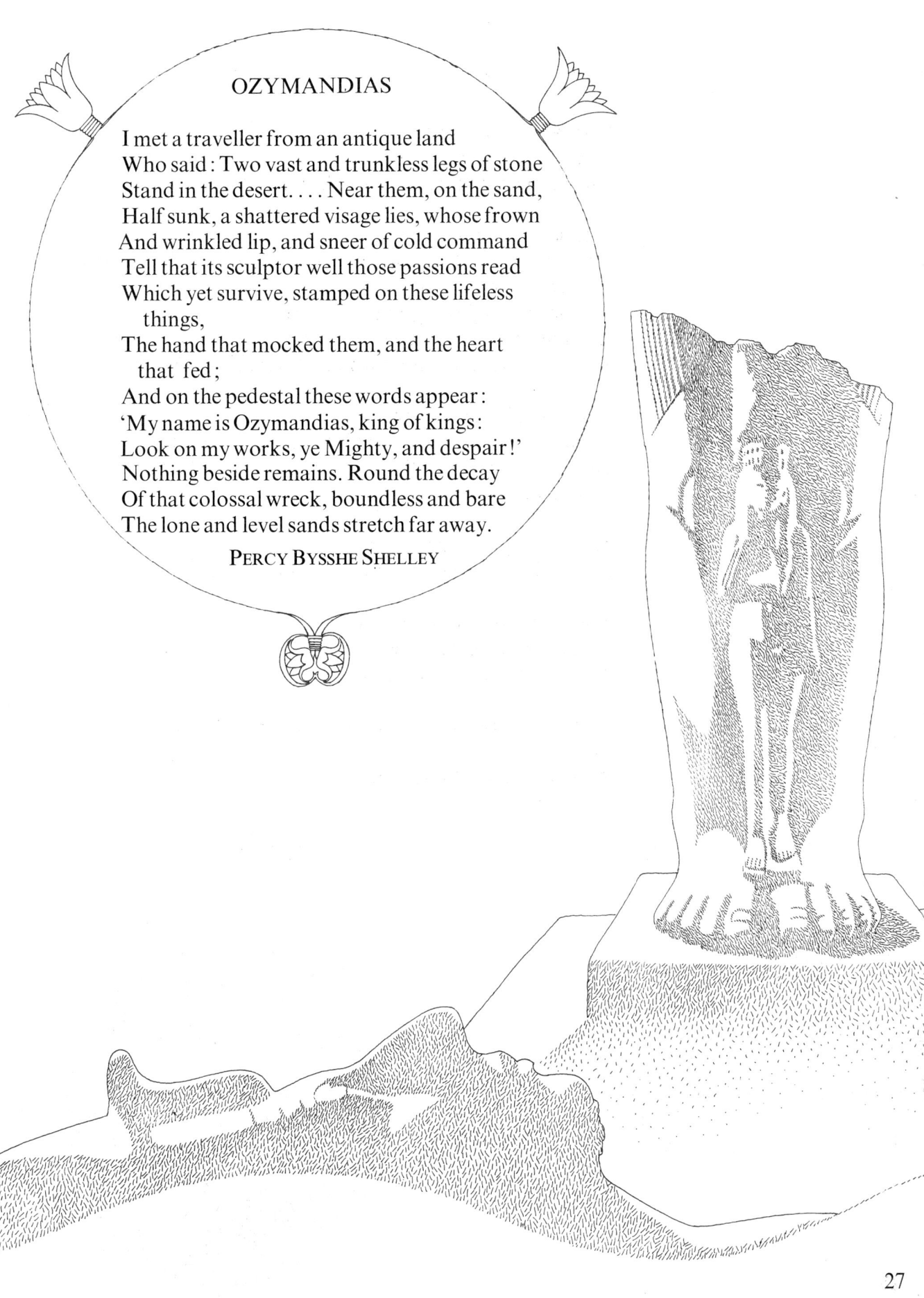

OZYMANDIAS

I met a traveller from an antique land
Who said : Two vast and trunkless legs of stone
Stand in the desert. . . . Near them, on the sand,
Half sunk, a shattered visage lies, whose frown
And wrinkled lip, and sneer of cold command
Tell that its sculptor well those passions read
Which yet survive, stamped on these lifeless
 things,
The hand that mocked them, and the heart
 that fed ;
And on the pedestal these words appear :
'My name is Ozymandias, king of kings :
Look on my works, ye Mighty, and despair !'
Nothing beside remains. Round the decay
Of that colossal wreck, boundless and bare
The lone and level sands stretch far away.

PERCY BYSSHE SHELLEY

THE REST OF THE DAY'S YOUR OWN

One day when I was out of work a job I went to seek,
To be a farmer's boy.
At last I found an easy job at half a crown a week,
To be a farmer's boy.
The farmer said, 'I think I've got the very job for you;
Your duties will be light, for this is all you've got to do:
Rise at three every morn, milk the cow with the crumpled
　　horn,
Feed the pigs, clean the sty, teach the pigeons the way to fly,
Plough the fields, mow the hay, help the cocks and hens to
　　lay,
Sow the seeds, tend the crops, chase the flies from the turnip
　　tops,
Clean the knives, black the shoes, scrub the kitchen and
　　sweep the flues,
Help the wife, wash the pots, grow the cabbages and
　　carrots,
Make the beds, dust the coals, mend the gramophone,
And then if there's no more work to do, the rest of the day's
　　your own.'

I scratched my head and thought it would be absolutely
　　prime
To be a farmer's boy.
The farmer said, 'Of course you'll have to do some overtime,
When you're a farmer's boy.'
Said he, 'The duties that I've given you, you'll be quickly
　　through,
So I've been thinking of a few more things that you can do;
Skim the milk, make the cheese, chop the meat for the
　　sausages,
Bath the kids, mend their clothes, use your face to scare the
　　crows,
In the milk, put the chalk, shave the knobs off the pickled
　　pork,

Shoe the horse, break the coal, take the cat for his midnight
   stroll,
Cook the food, scrub the stairs, teach the parrot to say his
   prayers,
Roast the joint, bake the bread, shake the feathers up in
   the bed,
When I have the gout, rub my funny bone,
And then if there's no more work to do, the rest of the day's
   your own.'

I thought it was a shame to take the money, you can bet,
To be a farmer's boy.
And so I wrote my duties down in case I should forget.
I was a farmer's boy.
It took all night to write 'em down, I didn't go to bed,
'But somehow I got all mixed up, and this is how they read:
Rise at three, every morn, milk the hen with the crumpled
   horn,
Scrub the farmer every day, teach the nanny goat how to lay,
Shave the cat, mend the cheese, fit the tights on the
   sausages,
Bath the pigs, break the pots, boil the kids with a few carrots,
Roast the horse, dust the bread, put the cocks and hens to
   bed,
Boots and shoes, black with chalk, shave the hair on the
   pickled pork,
All the rest I forgot, somehow it had flown,
But I got the sack this morning, so the rest of my life's my
   own.

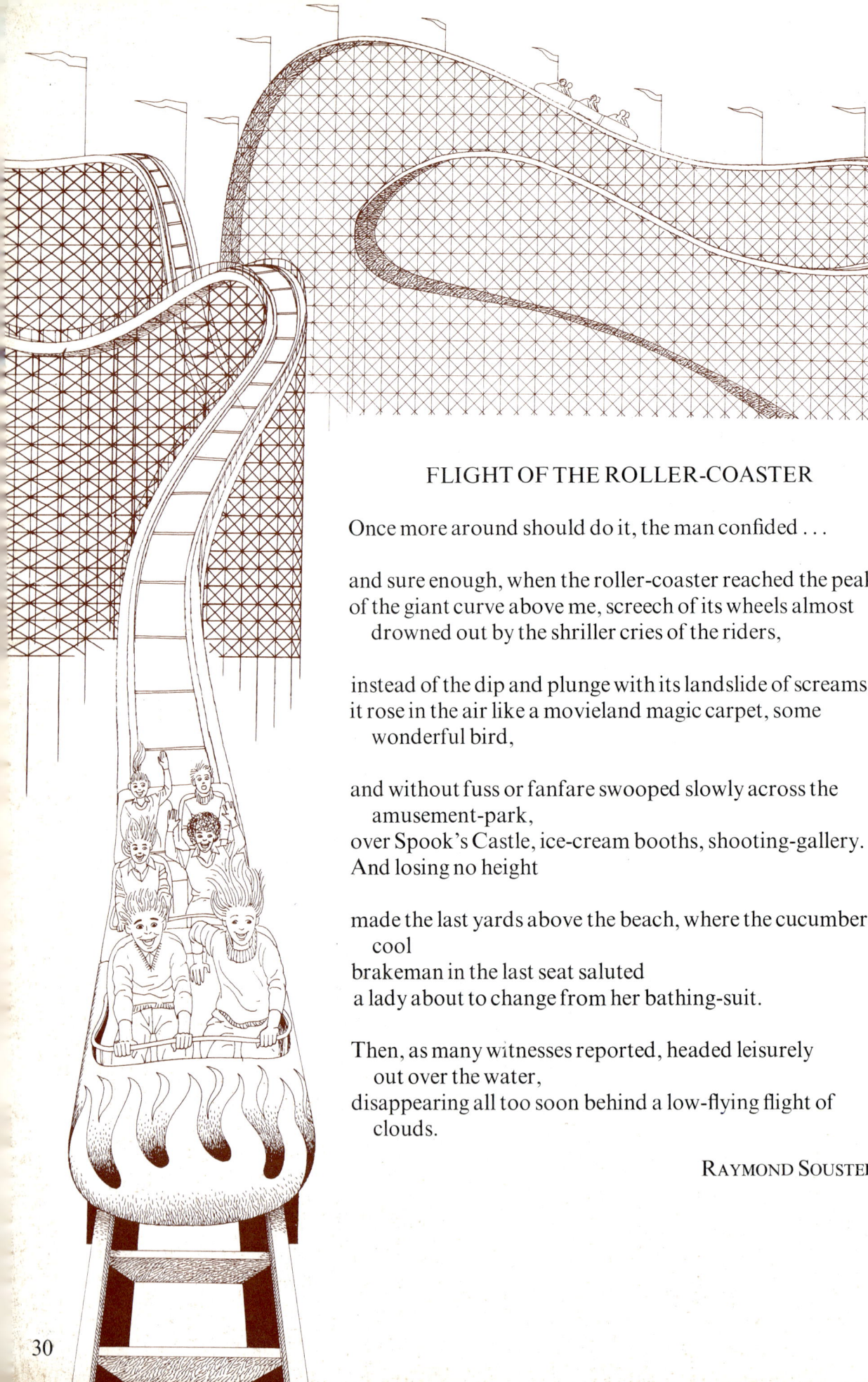

FLIGHT OF THE ROLLER-COASTER

Once more around should do it, the man confided . . .

and sure enough, when the roller-coaster reached the peak
of the giant curve above me, screech of its wheels almost
    drowned out by the shriller cries of the riders,

instead of the dip and plunge with its landslide of screams,
it rose in the air like a movieland magic carpet, some
    wonderful bird,

and without fuss or fanfare swooped slowly across the
    amusement-park,
over Spook's Castle, ice-cream booths, shooting-gallery.
And losing no height

made the last yards above the beach, where the cucumber-
    cool
brakeman in the last seat saluted
a lady about to change from her bathing-suit.

Then, as many witnesses reported, headed leisurely
    out over the water,
disappearing all too soon behind a low-flying flight of
    clouds.

RAYMOND SOUSTER

MAD AD

A Madison Avenue whizzkid
thought it a disgrace
That no one had exploited
the possibilities in space
Discussed it with a client
who agreed and very soon
A thousand miles of neontubing
were transported to the moon.

Now no one can ignore it
the product's selling fine
The night they turned the moon
into a Coca-Cola sign.

ROGER McGOUGH

Drink
Coca-Cola

31

SURPRISE! OR THE ESCAPOLOGIST

At the foot of the Apennine Mountains,
Where the astronauts explore,
The curious Lunar Sea-squirt
Watches from its door.

And as they wander blithely
Around in their lunar cars,
The Sea-squirt steals their module—
And flies away to Mars.

CAREY BLYTON

THE YOUNG LADY OF RIGA

There was a young lady of Riga
Who smiled as she rode on a Tiger;
    They came back from the ride
    With the lady inside,
And the smile on the face of the Tiger.

THE JUMBLIES

They went to sea in a Sieve, they did,
   In a Sieve they went to sea;
In spite of all their friends could say,
On a winter's morn, on a stormy day,
   In a Sieve they went to sea!
And when the Sieve turned round and round,
And everyone cried, 'You'll all be drowned!'
They called aloud, 'Our Sieve ain't big,
But we don't care a button, we don't care a fig!
   In a Sieve we'll go to sea.'
     Far and few, far and few,
       Are the lands where the Jumblies live;
     Their heads are green, and their hands are blue,
       And they went to sea in a Sieve.

They sailed away in a Sieve, they did,
   In a Sieve they sailed so fast;
With only a beautiful pea-green veil
Tied with a ribbon by way of a sail
   To a small tobacco-pipe mast;
And everyone said, who saw them go,
'O won't they be soon upset, you know,
For the sky is dark, and the voyage is long,
And happen what may, it's extremely wrong,
   In a Sieve to sail so fast.'
     Far and few, far and few,
       Are the lands where the Jumblies live;
     Their heads are green, and their hands are blue,
       And they went to sea in a Sieve.

The water it soon came in, it did,
     The water it soon came in;
So to keep them dry, they wrapped their feet
In a pinky paper, all folded neat,
     And they fastened it down with a pin.
And they passed the night in a crockery jar,
And each of them said, 'How wise we are!
Though the sky be dark and the voyage be long
Yet we never can think we were rash or wrong,
     While round in our Sieve we spin!'
          Far and few, far and few,
               Are the lands where the Jumblies live;
          Their heads are green, and their hands are blue,
          And they went to sea in a Sieve.

And all night long they sailed away;
     And when the sun went down,
They whistled and warbled a moony song,
To the echoing sound of a coppery gong,
     In the shade of the mountains brown.
'O Timballo! How happy we are,
When we live in a Sieve and a crockery jar,
And all night long in the moonlight pale,
We sail away with a pea-green sail
     In the shade of the mountains brown!'
          Far and few, far and few,
               Are the lands where the Jumblies live;
          Their heads are green, and their hands are blue,
          And they went to sea in a Sieve.

They sailed to the Western Sea, they did,
  To a land all covered with trees,
And they bought an Owl and a useful Cart,
And a pound of Rice and a Cranberry Tart,
  And a hive of silvery Bees.
And they bought a Pig, and some green Jack-daws,
And a lovely Monkey with lollipop paws,
And forty bottles of Ring-Bo-Ree,
  And no end of Stilton Cheese.
    Far and few, far and few,
      Are the lands where the Jumblies live;
    Their heads are green, and their hands are blue,
  And they went to sea in a Sieve.

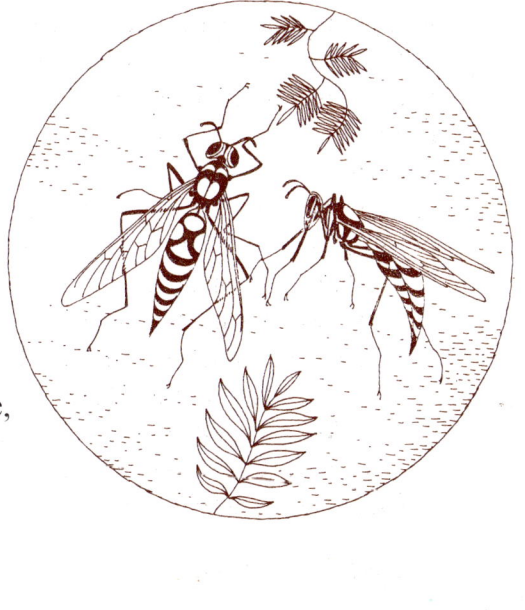

And in twenty years they all came back,
  In twenty years or more,
And every one said, 'How tall they've grown!
For they've been to the Lakes, and the Torrible Zone,
  And the hills of the Chankly Bore;'
And they drank their health and gave them a feast
Of dumplings made of beautiful yeast;
And everyone said, 'If we only live,
We, too, will go to sea in a Sieve—
  To the hills of the Chankly Bore!'
    Far and few, far and few,
      Are the lands where the Jumblies live;
    Their heads are green, and their hands are blue,
  And they went to sea in a Sieve.

EDWARD LEAR

35

JABBERWOCKY

'Twas brillig, and the slithy toves
   Did gyre and gimble in the wabe;
All mimsy were the borogoves,
   And the mome raths outgrabe.

'Beware the Jabberwock, my son!
   The jaws that bite, the claws that catch!
Beware the Jubjub bird, and shun
   The frumious Bandersnatch!'

He took his vorpal sword in hand:
   Long time the manxome foe he sought—
So rested he by the Tumtum tree,
   And stood awhile in thought.

And while in uffish thought he stood,
   The Jabberwock, with eyes of flame,
Came whiffling through the tulgey wood,
   And burbled as it came!

One, two! One, two! And through and through
   The vorpal blade went snicker-snack!
He left it dead, and with its head
   He went galumphing back.

'And hast thou slain the Jabberwock?
   Come to my arms, my beamish boy!'
O frabjous day! Callooh! Callay!'
   He chortled in his joy.

'Twas brillig, and the slithy toves
   Did gyre and gimble in the wabe:
All mimsy were the borogoves,
   And the mome raths outgrabe.

LEWIS CARROLL

THE LION AND ALBERT

There's a famous seaside place called Blackpool,
  That's noted for fresh air and fun,
And Mr. and Mrs. Ramsbottom
  Went there with young Albert, their son.

A grand little lad was young Albert,
  All dressed in his best; quite a swell
With a stick with an 'orse's 'ead 'andle,
  The finest that Woolworth's could sell.

They didn't think much to the Ocean:
  The waves, they was fiddlin' and small,
There was no wrecks and nobody drownded,
  Fact, nothing to laugh at at all.

So, seeking for further amusement,
  They paid and went into the Zoo,
Where they'd Lions and Tigers and Camels,
  And old ale and sandwiches too.

There were one great big Lion called Wallace;
  His nose were all covered with scars—
He lay in a somnolent posture
  With the side of his face on the bars.

Now Albert had heard about Lions,
  How they was ferocious and wild—
To see Wallace lying so peaceful,
  Well, it didn't seem right to the child.

So straightway the brave little feller,
  Not showing a morsel of fear,
Took his stick with its 'orse's 'ead 'andle
  And pushed it in Wallace's ear.

You could see that the Lion didn't like it,
    For giving a kind of a roll,
He pulled Albert inside the cage with 'im,
    And swallowed the little lad 'ole.

Then Pa, who had seen the occurrence,
    And didn't know what to do next,
Said 'Mother! Yon Lion's 'et Albert,'
    And Mother said 'Well, I am vexed!'

Then Mr. and Mrs. Ramsbottom—
    Quite rightly, when all's said and done—
Complained to the Animal Keeper
    That the Lion had eaten their son.

The keeper was quite nice about it;
    He said 'What a nasty mishap.
Are you sure that it's *your* boy he's eaten?'
    Pa said 'Am I sure? There's his cap!'

The manager had to be sent for.
    He came and he said 'What's to do?'
Pa said 'Yon Lion's 'et Albert,
    And 'im in his Sunday clothes, too.'

Then Mother said, 'Right's right, young feller;
    I think it's a shame and a sin
For a lion to go and eat Albert,
    And after we've paid to come in.'

The manager wanted no trouble,
    He took out his purse right away,
Saying 'How much to settle the matter?'
    And Pa said 'What do you usually pay?'

But Mother had turned a bit awkward
   When she thought where her Albert had gone.
She said 'No! someone's got to be summonsed'—
   So that was decided upon.

Then off they went to the P'lice Station,
   In front of the Magistrate chap;
They told 'im what happened to Albert,
   And proved it by showing his cap.

The Magistrate gave his opinion
   That no one was really to blame
And he said that he hoped the Ramsbottoms
   Would have further sons to their name.

At that Mother got proper blazing,
   'And thank you, sir, kindly,' said she.
'What, waste all our lives raising children
   To feed ruddy Lions? Not me!'

MARRIOTT EDGAR

THE SLITHERGADEE

The Slithergadee has crawled out of the sea;
He may catch all the others, but he won't catch me.
No, you won't catch me, old Slithergadee;
You may catch all the others, but you wo . . .

SHEL SILVERSTEIN

Taking a closer look

About the poems

Have you ever tried to describe an animal so that someone else can see exactly what it looks like? You will find it is almost as difficult as trying to describe another human being.

People often use comparisons with animals when talking about a person, and an animal may seem to have human characteristics. Even plants can be given human qualities—like the flowers in the poem **Lodged**.

The first poem in this section, **The Pasture**, is addressed by a grown-up to a child. The poet is trying to be reassuring, as if he knows that the child is probably a bit scared. And in the next poem, **Madam**, we see what it was that the child might have been scared of. The poet here looks back to his childhood, and remembers the terror and delight of having a new large animal about and how it changed things.

Ted Hughes, on the other hand, in **A March Calf**, tries to get right inside a young calf to show us how it might be feeling. At the same time he makes sure that we never stop looking at it as it really is—down to the last little quiver.

The Bear is a different kind of poem. The poet does not try to get inside the bear; he just watches him, trying to make us see exactly how he moves. Each time he uses a different way of describing the bear's movement—do you see what they are? And what does the bear seem to think of him?

The Hedgehog is different again: we are almost entirely outside the animal, and yet the poet makes us feel affection for him. Can you see how he does it?

John Wain's poem **The Gorilla** describes a gorilla in a cage and this time makes us think of him as if he were a man. What kind of man do you think he is though? A labouring man? A strong man? You might think so from the second stanza, but now look at the last two.

John Wain's gorilla is seen as a lazy animal; whereas **Weary Will** the wombat, who sounds from his name like a lazy animal, is about the most active animal in any of these poems, even though he only does one thing all the time.

Now look at the two poems describing lizards (**Gecko** and **The Lizard**). Which do you like best? Do you think one of them is better at showing what a lizard is really like?

Sea-weed and **Little Fish** are both by D. H. Lawrence. Notice how he says just one thing to catch the look of seaweed and one thing to describe the life of small fish in the sea. Can you write a short poem like that, saying just one thing about something to bring it alive?

It is not difficult to think of animals as being like humans, but when it comes to snails and worms you might think it was almost impossible.

Snails shows us one way in which snails are definitely not like us. Do you agree that it would be better if human beings were made this way?

In the case of worms we don't have to ask this question; although **Worms and the Wind** is about worms, it is much more about people. In what ways do we all behave like these worms?

The Fly looks at the way the world must seem to a small insect. **Serious Readers** on the other hand, looks at the way flies seem to us.

Now imagine yourself the size of Tom Thumb and you will understand how the tiny Lilliputian feels in **A Poem to Gulliver**. His view of Gulliver sounds just amusing—but it also shows how we sometimes respect things or people only because they are bigger than us.

If we had the senses of a tiny animal, we would hear things we don't usually hear as human beings. The man in **Lost Love** is seeing and hearing in this way, because he is so eager to find what he has lost. Reading the poem is rather like watching a film in which every tiny detail is magnified to many times its normal size.

This section includes a number of poems about the countryside and the way we look at it. In the past, country people were often looking for signs of the weather. They have handed down some of their best tips as little rhymes that are easy to remember. Of these, perhaps **Red Sky at Night** works best as a poem, because all the important words come in just the right places.

Of course we also go into the countryside to enjoy ourselves. Thomas Hardy's **Weathers** tries to get the feel of different kinds of weather by using very small details. In **The Spring** and **The Waking** too, we remember what it is like to go outside on a bright sunny day when the countryside seems as happy as we are.

In winter, the snow often makes everything look the same. But, as David McCord tells us, in **Snowflakes**, if you look at snowflakes under a microscope, no two flakes are the same. The world is full of things that we hardly stop to look at—like the dapples in Hopkins' **Pied Beauty**.

Now think about the first time you tried to ride a bicycle and then read **Esmé on her Brother's Bicycle**. Can you see anything that tells you the sort of girl she is? Poets notice things like this, and are always thinking of ways to describe them and pin them down. Like W. H. Davies, in **Leisure**, they find it worthwhile to stand and stare.

Even on a cold winter's night Robert Frost finds himself stopping to look into a wood. Try reading **Stopping by Woods** aloud, and you will see how often the poem goes on again, just when you think it might come to a stop. How does this help what he is saying?

In the last poem you will see how he sometimes enjoys making his words look awkward. **Neither out Far nor in Deep** is an odd title for a poem—but what he is talking about *is* odd: people by the sea tend to look out to sea rather than back at the land, even though there's much less to see.

This is a poem in which we take a closer look at the way other people look at the world—and see that this is sometimes much stranger than anything else that they, or we, are ever likely to see.

THE PASTURE

I'm going out to clean the pasture spring;
I'll only stop to rake the leaves away
(And wait to watch the water clear, I may):
I shan't be gone long.—You come too.

I'm going out to fetch the little calf
That's standing by the mother. It's so young,
It totters when she licks it with her tongue.
I shan't be gone long.—You come too.

ROBERT FROST

MADAM

One day grandfather came home with a calf
on a lead, grinning with his milk-white teeth.
Immediately we named her Madam, her hooves
clicked so much like high-heels in the courtyard.
'She'll give us milk in a year and a half,
and if she doesn't we'll slaughter her for beef,'
said grandfather, tying her under the guava leaves
in the garden. I stared and stared and stared,

and Madam stared back across the flower-bed.
I stood sucking a thumb and clutching the tail
of my nightshirt in the hot afternoon,
always on my toes and ready to run
to mother at the slightest turning of her head.
At evening I carried a bucket of meal
to Madam and with some confidence got within
a foot of touching her, and then I'd run

away carrying the smell of her sweating hide
to my pillow and the smell of her dung.
She would appear in my dreams dyed with red
pigment as for a festival, full grown
cow, her udders swaying from side to side
as she mooned away from the fields I'd hang
about in. The bizarre problems of childhood!
Ballooned in my nightshirt, I dreamed on.

No strategy could make Madam mine
as was the tricycle I rode or the thumb
which was sore with sucking. The dreams were
    hard-luck
stories. While Madam's sides bulged like a pear,
I ate fruit only of imagining,
touched her in thought. Where I went she
    wouldn't come.
Madam kicked me once in the stomach.
I suppose I shouldn't have gone so near.

ZULFIKAR GHOSE

A MARCH CALF

Right from the start he is dressed in his best—his
    blacks and his whites,
Little Fauntleroy—quiffed and glossy,
A Sunday suit, a wedding natty get-up,
Standing in dunged straw

Under cobwebby beams, near the mud wall,
Half of him legs,
Shining-eyed, requiring nothing more
But that mother's milk come back often.

Everything else is in order, just as it is.
Let the summer skies hold off, for the moment.
This is just as he wants it.
A little at a time, of each new thing, is best.

Too much and too sudden is too frightening—
When I block the light, a bulk from space,
To let him in to his mother for a suck,
He bolts a yard or two, then freezes,

Staring from every hair in all directions
Ready for the worst, shut up in his hopeful
    religion,
A little syllogism
With a wet blue-reddish muzzle, for God's thumb.

You see all his hopes bustling
As he reaches between the worn rails towards
The topheavy oven of his mother.
He trembles to grow, stretching his curl-tip
    tongue—

What did cattle ever find here
To make this dear little fellow
So eager to prepare himself?
He is already in the race, and quivering to win—

His new purpled eyeball swivel-jerks
In the elbowing push of his plans.
Hungry people are getting hungrier,
Butchers developing expertise and markets,

But he just wobbles his tail—and glistens
Within his dapper profile
Unaware of how his whole lineage
Has been tied up.

He shivers for feel of the world licking his side.
He is like an ember—one glow
Of lighting himself up
With the fuel of himself, breathing and
    brightening.

Soon he'll plunge out, to scatter his seething joy,
To be present at the grass,
To be free on the surface of such a wideness,
To find himself himself. To stand. To moo.

TED HUGHES

THE BEAR

His sullen shaggy-rimmed eyes followed my
　　every move,
Slowly gyrating they seemed to mimic the
　　movements of his massive head.
Similarly his body rolled unceasingly
From within.
As though each part possessed its own motion
And could think
And move for itself alone.
He had come forward in a lumbering, heavy spurt;
Like a beer barrel rolling down a plank.
The tremendous volume of his blood-red mouth
Yawned
So casually
But with so much menace.
And still the eye held yours.
So that you had to stay.
And then it turned.
Away.
So slowly.
Back
With that same motion
Back
To the bun-strewn
And honey-smelling back of its cage.

FREDERICK BROWN

HEDGEHOG

Twitching the leaves just where the drainpipe clogs
In ivy leaves and mud, a purposeful
Creature at night about its business. Dogs
Fear his stiff seriousness. He chews away

At beetles, worms, slugs, frogs. Can kill a hen
With one snap of his jaws, can taunt a snake
To death on muscled spines. Old countrymen
Tell tales of hedgehogs sucking a cow dry.

But this one, cramped by houses, fences, walls,
Must have slept here all winter in that heap
Of compost, or have inched by intervals
Through tidy gardens to this ivy bed.

And here, dim-eyed, but ears so sensitive
A voice within the house can make him freeze,
He scuffs the edge of danger: yet can live
Happily in our nights and absences.

A country creature, wary, quiet and shrewd,
He takes the milk we give him, when we're gone.
At night, our slamming voices must seem crude
To one who sits and waits for silences.

ANTHONY THWAITE

49

THE GORILLA

The gorilla lay on his back,
One hand cupped under his head,
Like a man.

Like a labouring man, tired with work,
A strong man with his strength burnt away
In the toil of earning a living.

Only of course he was not tired out with work,
Merely with boredom: his terrible strength
All burnt away by prodigal idleness.

A thousand days, and then a thousand days,
Idleness licked away his beautiful strength,
He having no need to earn a living.

It was all laid on, free of charge.
We maintained him, not for doing anything,
But for being what he was.

And so that Sunday morning he lay on his back,
Like a man, like a worn-out man,
One hand cupped under his terrible hard head.

Like a man, like a man,
One of those we maintain, not for doing anything,
But for being what they are.

A thousand days, and then a thousand days,
With everything laid on, free of charge,
They cup their heads in prodigal idleness.

JOHN WAIN
'*Au Jardin des Plantes*'

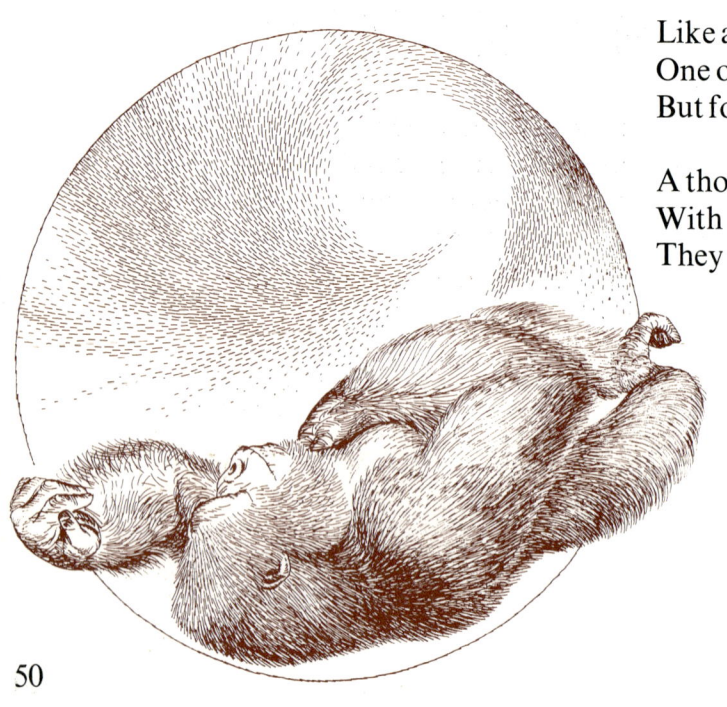

WEARY WILL

The strongest creature for his size
But least equipped for combat
That dwells beneath Australian skies
Is Weary Will the Wombat.

He digs his homestead underground,
He's neither shrewd nor clever;
For kangaroos can leap and bound
But wombats dig for ever.

The boundary-rider's netting fence
Excites his irritation;
It is to his untutored sense
His pet abomination.

And when to pass it he desires,
Upon his task he'll centre
And dig a hole beneath the wires,
Through which the dingoes enter.

And when to block the hole they strain
With logs and stones and rubble,
Bill Wombat digs it out again
Without the slightest trouble.

The boundary-rider bows to fate,
Admits he's made a blunder,
And rigs a little swinging gate
To let Bill Wombat under.

So most contentedly he goes
Between his haunt and burrow:
He does the only thing he knows,
And does it very thorough.

A. B. PATERSON

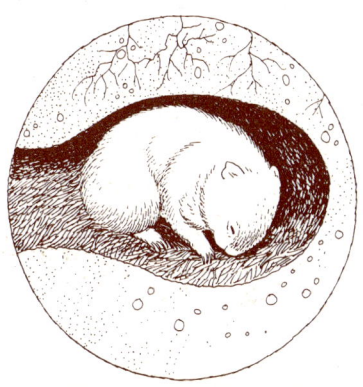

GECKO

There was a lizard kept me company
when I was in Gozo in the summer heat;
Gecko, they said he was—but to me
a lizard, fast, fleet—
'He'll bring you luck,' they told me.

Swift, pretty creature, my luck
was to have you there at all,
to watch you, now still as stone
then—a flick, a flip, and you were gone
fast as fury up the whitewashed wall,—
fly-prey snatched by your whip-crack tongue.

I loved your scaly pre-historic old-man's-face
with bulging eyes—pinpoints of light;
your suckered feet on plump doll's legs;
your tail, a graceful question mark.

Gecko, entrancing guest, you brought
an ancient beauty to my bare white wall.

NOEL LLOYD

THE LIZARD

He too has eaten well—
I can see that by the distended pulsing middle;
And his world and mine are the same,
The Mediterranean sun shining on us, equally,
His head, stiff as a scarab, turned to one side,
His right eye staring straight at me,
One leaf-like foot hung laxly
Over the worn curb of the terrace,
The tail straight as an awl,
Then suddenly flung up and over,
Ending curled around and over again,
A thread-like firmness.

(Would a cigarette disturb him?)

At the first scratch of the match
He turns his head slightly,
Retiring to nudge his neck half-way under
A dried strawberry leaf,
His tail grey with the ground now,
One round eye still toward me.
A white cabbage-butterfly drifts in,
Bumbling up and around the bamboo windbreak;
But the eye of the tiny lizard stays with me.
One greenish lid lifts a bit higher,
Then slides down over the eye's surface,
Rising again, slowly,
Opening, closing.

To whom does this terrace belong?—
With its limestone crumbling into fine greyish
    dust,
Its bevy of bees, and its wind-beaten rickety
    sun-chairs.
Not to me, but this lizard,
Older than I, or the cockroach.

THEODORE ROETHKE

53

SEA-WEED

Sea-weed sways and sways and swirls
as if swaying were its form of stillness;
and if it flushes against fierce rock
it slips over it as shadows do, without hurting itself.

D. H. LAWRENCE

LITTLE FISH

The tiny fish enjoy themselves
in the sea
Quick little splinters of life,
their little lives are fun to them
in the sea.

D. H. LAWRENCE

THE BABY BLACKBIRD

With head lolling on its fat body,
The baby dozed in sleepy sunlight,
    A few downy feathers,
Like thistle seeds, waving aimlessly in the wind.

The snake-skin eye-lids, like a pelican's great beak,
    Covered the beady eyes:
But as a pigeon cooed lazily,
One lid revealed a deep blue pool of curiosity,
Which was concealed again after one bored blink.

The bird rocked precariously,
Then wobbled over the edge of the fence
Deflated, on the grass, with fast heart-beat,
It tottered unsteadily to its skeleton feet.

CHRISTINE
aged 15

LODGED

The rain to the wind said,
'You push and I'll pelt.'
They so smote the garden bed
That the flowers actually knelt,
And lay lodged—though not dead.
I know how the flowers felt.

ROBERT FROST

SNAILS

Snails are hermaphrodite
(Which doesn't mean they hunt at night
Or that baby snails are excessively fat
No, it doesn't mean anything like that)
It means something like this;
    First they kiss
        Then they mate
            Then they separate
                Then they BOTH reproduce
To some people this idea may be new
But I can vouch it's perfectly true
If only God had had the foresight
To make us all hermaphrodite!

DOMINIC HODGKIN
aged 12

56

WORMS AND THE WIND

Worms would rather be worms.
Ask a worm and he says, 'Who knows what a
    worm knows?'
Worms go down and up and over and under.
Worms like tunnels.
When worms talk they talk about the worm world.
Worms like it in the dark.
Neither the sun nor the moon interests a worm.
Zigzag worms hate circle worms.
Curve worms never trust square worms.
Worms know what worms want.
Slide worms are suspicious of crawl worms.
One worm asks another, 'How does your belly
    drag today?'
The shape of a crooked worm satisfies a crooked
    worm.
A straight worm says, 'Why not be straight?'
Worms tired of crawling begin to slither.
Long worms slither farther than short worms.
Middle-sized worms say, 'It is nice to be neither
    long nor short.'
Old worms teach young worms to say, 'Don't be
    sorry for me unless you have been a worm and
    lived in worm places and read worm books.'
When worms go to war they dig in, come out and
    fight, dig in again, come out and fight again,
    dig in again, and so on.
Worms underground never hear the wind
    overground and sometimes they ask, 'What is
    this wind we hear of?'

CARL SANDBURG

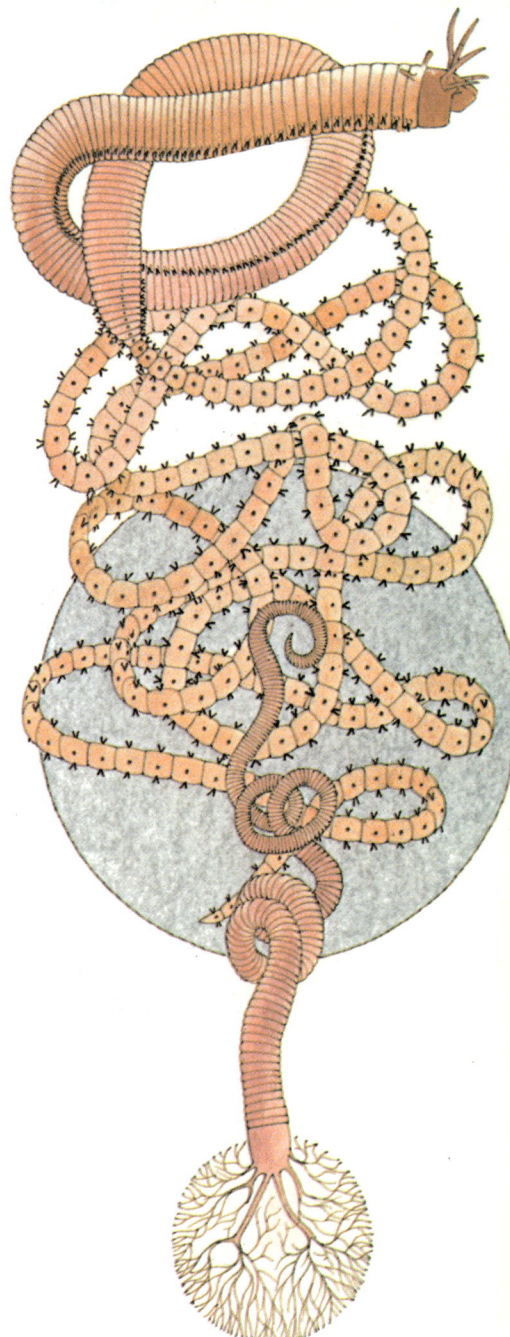

THE FLY

How large unto the tiny fly
  Must little things appear!—
A rosebud like a feather bed,
  Its prickle like a spear;

A dewdrop like a looking-glass,
  A hair like golden wire;
The smallest grain of mustard-seed
  As fierce as coals of fire;

A loaf of bread, a lofty hill;
  A wasp, a cruel leopard;
And specks of salt as bright to see
  As lambkins to a shepherd.

WALTER DE LA MARE

58

SERIOUS READERS

All the flies are reading microscopic books;
They hold themselves quite tense and silent
With shoulders hunched, legs splayed out
On the white formica table-top, reading.
With my book I slide into the diner-booth;
They rise and circle and settle again, reading
With hunched corselets. They do not attempt
   to taste
Before me my fat hamburger-plate, but wait,
Like courteous readers until I put it to one side,
Then taste briefly and resume their tomes
Like reading-stands with horny specs. I
Read as I eat, one fly
Alights on my book, the size of print;
I let it be. Read and let read.

PETER REDGROVE

SARDINES

A baby sardine
Saw her first submarine:
She was scared and watched through a peephole.

'Oh, come, come, come,'
Said the sardine's mum,
'It's only a tin full of people.'

SPIKE MILLIGAN

A LILLIPUTIAN WRITES
A POEM TO GULLIVER

See! and believe your Eyes!

    See him stride
Vallies wide:
Over Woods,
Over Floods.
When he treads,
Mountains Heads
Groan and shake;
Armies quake,
Lest his Spurn
Overturn
Man and Steed:
Troops take Heed!
Left and Right,
Speed your Flight!
Lest an Host
Beneath his Foot be lost.

    Turn'd aside
From his Hide,
Safe from Wound
Darts rebound.
From his Nose
Clouds he blows;
When he speaks,
Thunder breaks!
When he eats,
Famine threats;
When he drinks,
Neptune shrinks!
Nigh thy Ear,
In Mid Air,
On thy Hand
Let me stand,
So shall I,
Lofty Poet! touch the Sky.

ALEXANDER POPE
*from 'Verses on
Gulliver's Travels'*

60

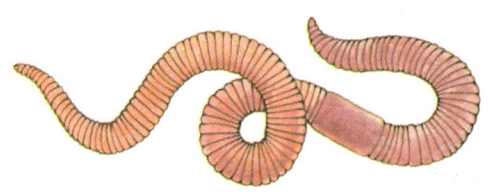

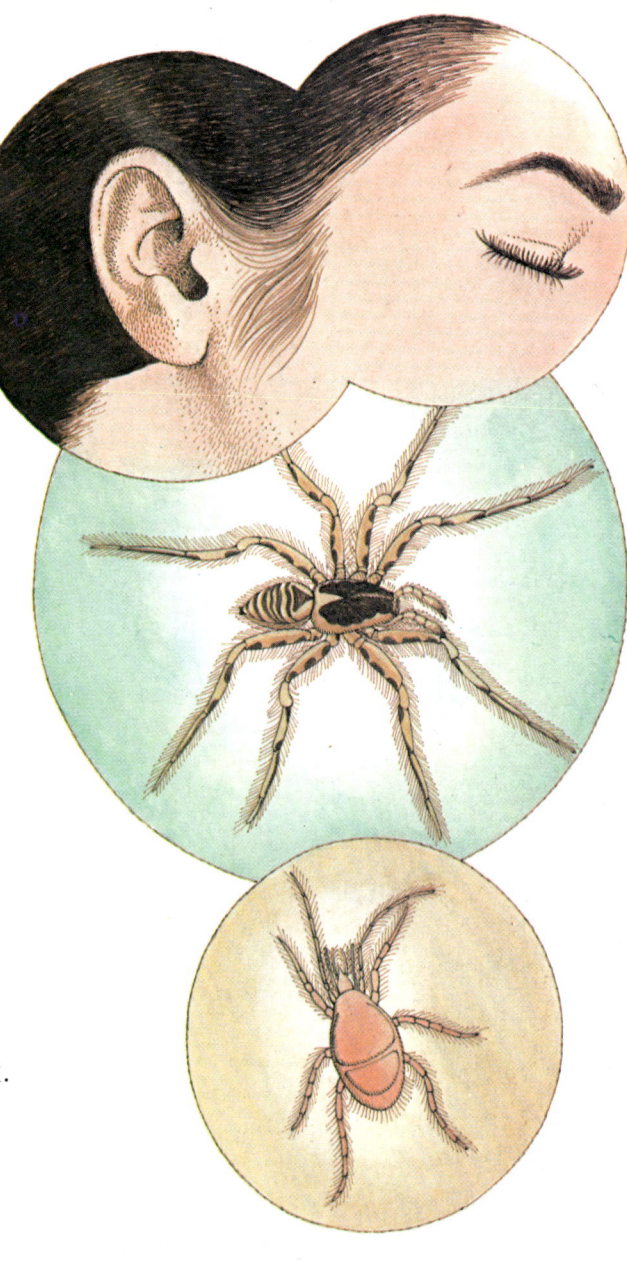

LOST LOVE

His eyes are quickened so with grief,
He can watch a grass or leaf
Every instant grow; he can
Clearly through a flint wall see,
Or watch the startled spirit flee
From the throat of a dead man.

    Across two counties he can hear,
And catch your words before you speak.
The woodlouse, or the maggot's weak
Clamour rings in his sad ear;
And noise so slight it would surpass
Credence:—drinking sound of grass,
Worm talk, clashing jaws of moth
Chumbling holes in cloth:
The groan of ants who undertake
Gigantic loads for honour's sake,
Their sinews creak, their breath comes thin:
Whir of spiders when they spin,
And minute whispering, mumbling, sighs
Of idle grubs and flies.

    This man is quickened so with grief,
He wanders god-like or like thief
Inside and out, below, above,
Without relief seeking lost love.

ROBERT GRAVES

THE WEATHER FORECAST

Rain, rain, go away,
Come again another day—
Not a public holiday!

Red sky at night,
Shepherd's delight;
Red sky in the morning,
Shepherd's warning.

When clouds appear
Like rocks and towers,
The earth's refreshed
By frequent showers.

Evening red and morning grey
Send the traveller on his way;
Evening grey and morning red
Bring the rain upon his head.

When the wind is in the east,
It's good for neither man nor beast;
When the wind is in the north,
The fisherman he goes not forth;
When the wind is in the south,
It blows the bait in the fishes' mouth;
When the wind is in the west,
Then it's at the very best.

When the dew is on the grass,
Rain will never come to pass.

WEATHERS

This is the weather the cuckoo likes,
    And so do I;
When showers betumble the chestnut spikes,
    And nestlings fly:
And the little brown nightingale bills his best,
And they sit outside at 'The Travellers' Rest',
And maids come forth sprig-muslin drest,
And citizens dream of the south and west,
    And so do I.

This is the weather the shepherd shuns,
    And so do I;
When beeches drip in browns and duns,
    And thresh, and ply;
And hill-hid tides throb, throe on throe,
And meadow rivulets overflow,
And drops on gate-bars hang in a row,
And rooks in families homeward go,
    And so do I.

THOMAS HARDY

THE SPRING

Now that the Winter's gone, the earth hath lost
Her snow-white robes; and now no more the frost
Candies the grass, or casts an icy cream
Upon the silver lake or crystal stream:
But the warm sun thaws the benumbed earth,
And makes it tender; gives a sacred birth
To the dead swallow; wakes in hollow tree
The drowsy cuckoo and the humble bee.
Now do a choir of chirping minstrels bring
In triumph to the world the youthful Spring:
The valleys, hills, and woods in rich array
Welcome the coming of the longed-for May.

THOMAS CAREW

THE WAKING

I strolled across
An open field;
The sun was out;
Heat was happy.

This way! This way!
The wren's throat shimmered,
Either to other,
The blossoms sang.

The stones sang,
The little ones did,
And flowers jumped
Like small goats.

A ragged fringe
Of daisies waved;
I wasn't alone
In a grove of apples.

Far in the wood
A nestling sighed;
The dew loosened
Its morning smells.

I came where the river
Ran over stones:
My ears knew
An early joy.

And all the waters
Of all the streams
Sang in my veins
That summer day.

THEODORE ROETHKE

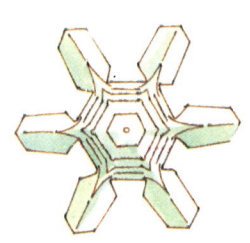

SNOWFLAKES

Sometime this winter if you go
To walk in soft new-falling snow
When flakes are big and come down slow

To settle on your sleeve as bright
As stars that couldn't wait for night
You won't know what you have in sight—

Another world—unless you bring
A magnifying glass. This thing
We call a snowflake is the king

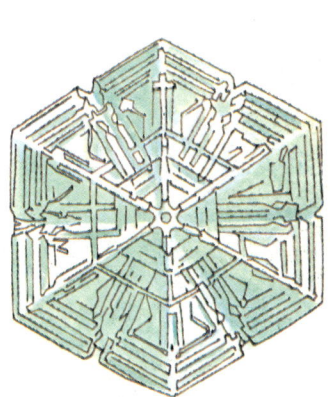

Of crystals. Do you like surprise?
Examine him three times his size:
At first you won't believe your eyes.

Stars look alike, but flakes do not:
No two the same in all the lot
That you will get in any spot

You chance to be, for every one
Come spinning through the sky has none
But his own window-wings of sun:

Joints, points, and crosses. What could make
Such lacework with no crack or break?
In billion billions, no mistake?

DAVID McCORD

OBITUARY ON THE DEMOLITION OF A HOUSE IN GROVE LANE, CAMBERWELL

On the first day
I saw a woman
Dressed in a jumble sale
Eating a meal at four o'clock
She sat on the steps
And I felt sorry for her
And the house.

On the second day
There were no windows
And in place of a roof
A dull, grey sky:
The men had come
To demolish.

On the third day
It was a hollow shell,
The wall-paper brown-stained
Torn and peeling
Could be seen by all
—But no-one stopped to look.

On the fourth day
There was smoke in the air
Dust around us
The stone crashed around us
And there were men with dirty faces
And it went.

Today
It was a hole
I stopped to see
The sand and rotten wood:
The broken bricks
And solemn cavity
That was once a house.
But no-one seemed concerned.

MARIA DAWSON
aged 15

THE DESERTED HOUSE

There's no smoke in the chimney,
    And the rain beats on the floor;
There's no glass in the window,
    There's no wood in the door;
The heather grows behind the house,
    And the sand lies before.

No hand hath trained the ivy,
    The walls are gray and bare;
The boats upon the sea sail by,
    Nor ever tarry there.
No beast of the field comes nigh,
    Nor any bird of the air.

MARY COLERIDGE

AFTER SPENDING A NIGHT ALONE, AT THE COTTAGE OF A CERTAIN MR. WANG AT PO-SHAN

Hungry rats race around my bed;
Bats tumble and dance in lamplight.
Upon the roof, among the pines, wind spouts
incessant rain
While tattered paper flaps against the window,
talks to itself.

North of the border, south of the Yangtze, no
    stranger to me;
Now I am home, grey haired, ashen faced—
Cotton quilt, autumn night, and I lie awake;
Ten thousand miles of rivers and hills pass before
my eyes.

HSIN CH'I-CHI

67

LEISURE

What is this life if, full of care,
We have no time to stand and stare?

No time to stand beneath the boughs
And stare as long as sheep or cows.

No time to see, when woods we pass,
Where squirrels hide their nuts in grass.

No time to see, in broad daylight,
Streams full of stars, like skies at night.

No time to turn at Beauty's glance,
And watch her feet, how they can dance.

No time to wait till her mouth can
Enrich that smile her eyes began.

A poor life this if, full of care,
We have no time to stand and stare.

WILLIAM H. DAVIES

ESMÉ ON HER BROTHER'S BICYCLE

One foot on, one foot pushing, Esmé starting off beside
Wheels too tall to mount astride,
Swings the off leg forward featly,
Clears the high bar nimbly, neatly,
With a concentrated frown
Bears the upper pedal down
As the lower rises, then
Brings her whole weight round again,
Leaning forward, gripping tight,
With her knuckles showing white,
Down the road goes, fast and small,
Never sitting down at all.

RUSSELL HOBAN

PIED BEAUTY

Glory be to God for dappled things—
    For skies of couple-colour as a brinded cow;
      For rose-moles all in stipple upon trout that swim;
Fresh-firecoal chestnut-falls; finches' wings;
    Landscape plotted and pieced—fold, fallow, and plough;
      And all trades, their gear and tackle and trim.

All things counter, original, spare, strange;
    Whatever is fickle, freckled (who knows how?)
      With swift, slow; sweet, sour; adazzle, dim;
He fathers-forth whose beauty is past change:
        Praise him.

GERARD MANLEY HOPKINS

STOPPING BY WOODS
ON A SNOWY EVENING

Whose woods these are I think I know.
His house is in the village though;
He will not see me stopping here
To watch his woods fill up with snow.

My little horse must think it queer
To stop without a farmhouse near
Between the woods and frozen lake
The darkest evening of the year.

He gives his harness bells a shake
To ask if there is some mistake.
The only other sound's the sweep
Of easy wind and downy flake.

The woods are lovely, dark and deep.
But I have promises to keep,
And miles to go before I sleep,
And miles to go before I sleep.

ROBERT FROST

NEITHER OUT FAR NOR IN DEEP

The people along the sand
All turn and look one way.
They turn their back on the land.
They look at the sea all day.

As long as it takes to pass
A ship keeps raising its hull;
The wetter ground like glass
Reflects a standing gull.

The land may vary more;
But wherever the truth may be—
The water comes ashore,
And the people look at the sea.

They cannot look out far.
They cannot look in deep.
But when was that ever a bar
To any watch they keep?

ROBERT FROST

Heroes and Victims

About the poems

If you turn the next page you will find two poems about heroes. When you have read them you will have several things to think about. Are heroes people we want to be like? Do boys and girls have the same sort of heroes? What would a poem called 'My Heroine' be like? (You might try and write one.)

When we talk about heroes, and victims, we are often talking about ourselves. We are also talking about power and the way it works in life. Most of us enjoy the **Superman** feeling —even if we know that our dreams of power are more like those of the inventor in **Supermarine**.

The teacher in **He Who Owns the Whistle** likes the way that everything falls into place when he blows his 'Acme Thunderer'. But we are all of us sometimes powerless in new places we don't quite understand, like the child in **First Day at School**. Do you think that new children usually feel like the one in the poem?

In the animal world too, there are natural heroes—and natural victims. It is difficult not to think of Tennyson's **Eagle** as a hero and Chesterton's **Donkey** as a victim. But even the donkey likes to think of himself as a hero, and remembers one moment when he *was*. (If you don't know when that was look at Chapter 21 of *St. Matthew's Gospel*.)

Like the eagle, Blake's **Tyger** is obviously a hero and we admire him. But at the end there is a question ('did he who made the Lamb make thee?') which reminds us that the tiger we admire has his victims—and has no mercy on them.

In **Hello Mr Python**, Spike Milligan looks at a snake which is not as obviously heroic but which has its victims too. Notice how differently the two poems on these two pages are written. How does this fit their meanings?

Now back to human heroes. **The Big Sleeper** is a funny poem which shows how you can sound strong when you are not, by using the language of strong men. (Even when talking about something very unheroic like lying in bed.)

In **The Bully Asleep** on the other hand, Bill Craddock is strong—but not heroic at all. The poet points out that strong people can sometimes become victims, as Bill does here—even though the other children will become *his* victims again when he wakes up.

Thinking about strength and weakness in these ways should remind us of the way we treat animals. When American Indians think about hunting, they do not feel very sympathetic towards their victims. Yet, in the second of the **Hunting Songs**, they describe what hunting must seem like to the deer and so make us feel sorry for it.

Other poets feel more directly sympathetic towards animal victims. Shakespeare, in **The Hunted Hare**, describes the hare's plight very exactly, and he also makes us think what it is like to be a human victim; while James Stephens in **The Snare** describes how it is when we feel sympathy for an animal victim and can do nothing to help.

Is the hawk in Ted Hughes' **Hawk Roosting** a hero? Heroism usually means taking risks, but the hawk doesn't want to risk anything; he wants to keep things just as they are and believes that he has the power and the right to do so. The hawk's arrogance—or stern belief that he is right—may remind us of people we know, and perhaps of ourselves in certain moods. In **A Poison Tree**, Blake shows how nasty and mean-minded this feeling can make us. (Try reading the poem aloud, very slowly and gloatingly.)

People are not always like this however. They may express their anger more directly—like the North Africans described in **Fighting Frenzy** who rush straight into battle.

On the other hand, people who work with growing things are usually much gentler; they realize that the most lasting kind of power is to be found in nature. **The Woman's Song** is a poem of delight in the power of corn as it begins to grow towards harvest. In **Transplanting**, the poet marvels at the way in which, with the help of gentle fingers, weak young plants will soon grow strong—ready to produce more young plants again.

We see the power of the human hand again in **My Dad's Thumb**, though this time in a comic kind of way. And in **The Picnic in Jammu** we see how, in a family, power (in this case the strength of Uncle Ayub) can be playful rather than frightening.

Jamaican Fisherman and **The Lament of the Banana Man** taken together, show how one Jamaican can seem a hero when he is at home with his fishing gear; while another can seem a victim when he is working as a ticket-collector in a faraway London. But is the ticket-collector really a victim? Isn't he better off in some ways than the fisherman? How does he think of himself?

Now look at the children in **The Park**. Are they victims? And what about **Grandfather**? Does the person who is speaking in this poem remember him as a hero or a victim?

The next three poems are also about death—which makes us all its victims in the end. Yet although the dying cowboy in **The Cowboy's Lament** looks at first like a victim, he has led an exciting life and was loved by his friends—so that he appears more as a hero by the end.

The **Lyke-Wake Dirge**, a strongly religious poem, reminds us that the way we behave towards victims in this world may affect what happens to us after death.

A Land Dirge returns to the subject of the power of nature, pointing out how, after death, we are completely at its mercy—however powerful we may have been during our lives.

The next poem, **As it Was**, is about the way we sometimes just pity people in trouble instead of helping them; later we may regret that we thought 'it was not our concern'. What do you think has happened in this poem? Are we meant to know?

The small boy in **At the Railway Station** has no money to give to someone in trouble, but he gives something much more. What do you think this is?

Finally we turn to **The Fiddler of Dooney**. Do you feel he is a hero or a victim? What are we to call such a man who has this strange power and who uses it so gently? Is he the strongest of our heroes? Or is he not really a hero at all? What do you think?

A HERO

My hero is D. Dougan,
He wears old gold and black.
He goes through all defenders,
He leads the Wolves attack.

He scores in nearly every game,
He thrills the north bank choir.
He kicks the ball right through the net,
Just like a ball of fire.

JOHN LANE
aged 12

ANOTHER HERO

Clothed in black he rides through the night,
He bids me a farewell and gallops away,
The horses' shoes I can hear fading in the distance,
Everything is quiet and I feel sad,
Shall I ever see him again?
I turn away to my cottage which now looks like a
    sad white dog,
And the honeysuckle like drooping chains,
I think of the darkness,
And of my hero.

ANNE MARIE HANCOCK
aged 11

SUPERMAN

I drive my car to supermarket,
The way I take is superhigh,
A superlot is where I park it,
And Super Suds are what I buy.

Supersalesmen sell me tonic—
Super-Tone-O, for Relief.
The planes I ride are supersonic.
In trains, I like the Super Chief.

Supercilious men and women
Call me superficial—me
Who so superbly learned to swim in
Supercolossality.

Superphosphate-fed foods feed me;
Superservice keeps me new.
Who would dare to supersede me,
Super-super-superwho?

JOHN UPDIKE

SUPERMARINE

As they fished his old plane from the sea
The inventor just chortled with glee.
 'I shall build,' and he laughed,
  'A submarine craft,
And perhaps it will fly. We shall see.'

HE WHO OWNS THE WHISTLE,
RULES THE WORLD

january wind and the sun
playing truant again.
Rain beginning to scratch
its fingernails across
the blackboard sky

in the playground
kids divebomb, corner
at silverstone or execute
traitors. Armed
with my Acme Thunderer
I step outside,
take a deep breath
and bring the world
to a standstill

ROGER McGOUGH

FIRST DAY AT SCHOOL

A millionbillionwillion miles from home
Waiting for the bell to go. (To go where?)
Why are they all so big, other children?
So noisy? So much at home they
must have been born in uniform
Lived all their lives in playgrounds
Spent the years inventing games
that don't let me in. Games
that are rough, that swallow you up.

And the railings.
All around, the railings.
Are they to keep out wolves and monsters?
Things that carry off and eat children?
Things you don't take sweets from?
Perhaps they're to stop us getting out
Running away from the lessins. Lessin.
What does a lessin look like?
Sounds small and slimy.
They keep them in glassrooms.
Whole rooms made out of glass. Imagine.

I wish I could remember my name
Mummy said it would come in useful.
Like wellies. When there's puddles.
Yellowwellies. I wish she was here.
I think my name is sewn on somewhere
Perhaps the teacher will read it for me.
Tea-cher. The one who makes the tea.

ROGER McGOUGH

THE EAGLE

He clasps the crag with crooked hands
Close to the sun in lonely lands,
Ringed with the azure world, he stands.

The wrinkled sea beneath him crawls;
He watches from his mountain walls,
And like a thunderbolt he falls.

ALFRED, LORD TENNYSON

THE DONKEY

When fishes flew and forests walked
    And figs grew upon thorn,
Some moment when the moon was blood
    Then surely I was born.

With monstrous head and sickening cry
    And ears like errant wings,
The devil's walking parody
    On all four-footed things.

The tattered outlaw of the earth,
    Of ancient crooked will;
Starve, scourge, deride me: I am dumb,
    I keep my secret still.

Fools! For I also had my hour;
    One far fierce hour and sweet:
There was a shout about my ears,
    And palms before my feet.

G. K. CHESTERTON

THE TYGER

Tyger! Tyger! burning bright
In the forests of the night,
What immortal hand or eye
Could frame thy fearful symmetry?

In what distant deeps or skies
Burnt the fire of thine eyes?
On what wings dare he aspire?
What the hand dare seize the fire?

And what shoulder, and what art,
Could twist the sinews of thy heart?
And when thy heart began to beat,
What dread hand? and what dread feet?

What the hammer? what the chain?
In what furnace was thy brain?
What the anvil? what dread grasp
Dare its deadly terrors clasp?

When the stars threw down their spears,
And watered heaven with their tears,
Did he smile his work to see?
Did he who made the Lamb make thee?

Tyger! Tyger! burning bright
In the forests of the night,
What immortal hand or eye
Dare frame thy fearful symmetry?

WILLIAM BLAKE

HELLO MR PYTHON

Hello Mr Python
Curling round a tree,
Bet you'd like to make yourself
A dinner out of me

Can't you change your habits
Crushing people's bones?
I wouldn't like a dinner
That emitted fearful groans.

SPIKE MILLIGAN

THE BULLY ASLEEP

This afternoon, when grassy
Scents through the classroom crept,
Bill Craddock laid his head
Down on his desk, and slept.

The children came round him:
Jimmy, Roger, and Jane;
They lifted his head timidly
And let it sink again.

'Look, he's gone sound asleep, Miss,'
Said Jimmy Adair;
'He stays up all the night, you see;
His mother doesn't care.'

'Stand away from him children.'
Miss Andrews stooped to see.
'Yes, he's asleep; go on
With your writing, and let him be.'

'Now's a good chance!' whispered Jimmy;
And he snatched Bill's pen and hid it.
'Kick him under the desk, hard;
He won't know who did it.'

'Fill all his pockets with rubbish—
Paper, apple-cores, chalk.'
So they plotted, while Jane
Sat wide-eyed at their talk.

Not caring, not hearing,
Bill Craddock he slept on;
Lips parted, eyes closed—
Their cruelty gone.

'Stick him with pins!' muttered Roger.
'Ink down his neck!' said Jim.
But Jane, tearful and foolish,
Wanted to comfort him.

JOHN WALSH

I'M THE BIG SLEEPER

I'm the big sleeper
rolled up in his sheets
at the break of day

I'm a big sleeper living soft
in a hard kind of way

The light through the curtain
can't wake me
I'm under the blankets

you can't shake me
the pillow rustler
and blanket gambler
a mean tough eiderdown man

I keep my head
I stay in bed.

MICHAEL ROSEN

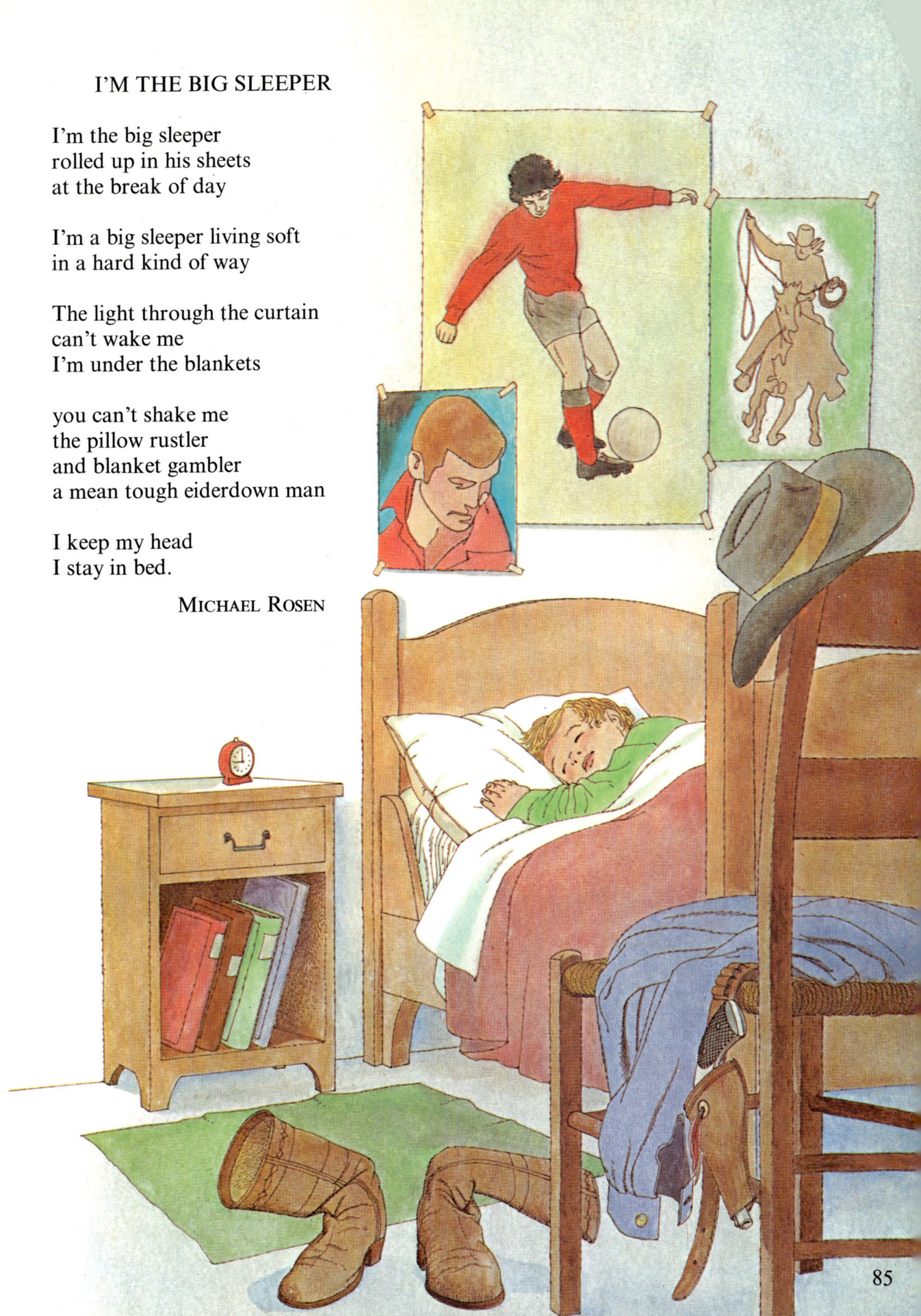

85

HUNTING SONG

One I have wounded, yonder he moves,
Yonder he moves, bleeding at the mouth.

One I have wounded, yonder he moves,
Yonder he moves, with staggering steps.

One I have wounded, yonder he moves,
Yonder he falls, yonder he falls.

North American Indians

HUNTING SONG

(*The deer speaks:*)
Lo, surely I shall die.
Over there, toward the west,
Here and there I went running.
Over there in the west
It thundered; it shook me.

Lo, surely I shall die.
Over there, toward the east,
Here and there I went running.
Over there, in the east,
It echoed, it threw me down.

Californian Indians

THE HUNTED HARE

'By this, poor hare, far off upon a hill,
Stands on his hinder legs with listening ear,
To hearken if his foes pursue him still:
Anon their loud alarms he doth hear;
   And now his grief may be compared well
   To one sore sick that hears the passing-bell.

'Then shalt thou see the dew-bedabbled wretch
Turn, and return, indenting with the way;
Each envious brier his weary legs doth scratch,
Each shadow makes him stop, each murmur stay:
   For misery is trodden on by many,
   And being low never relieved by any.'

WILLIAM SHAKESPEARE

THE SNARE

I hear a sudden cry of pain!
   There is a rabbit in a snare:
Now I hear the cry again,
   But I cannot tell from where.

But I cannot tell from where
   He is calling out for aid;
Crying on the frightened air,
   Making everything afraid.

Making everything afraid,
   Wrinkling up his little face,
As he cries again for aid;
   And I cannot find the place!

And I cannot find the place
   Where his paw is in the snare:
Little one! Oh, little one!
   I am searching everywhere.

JAMES STEPHENS

HAWK ROOSTING

I sit in the top of the wood, my eyes closed.
Inaction, no falsifying dream
Between my hooked head and hooked feet:
Or in sleep rehearse perfect kills and eat.

The convenience of the high trees!
The air's buoyancy and the sun's ray
Are of advantage to me;
And the earth's face upward for my inspection.

My feet are locked upon the rough bark.
It took the whole of Creation
To produce my foot, my each feather:
Now I hold Creation in my foot

Or fly up, and revolve it all slowly—
I kill where I please because it is all mine.
There is no sophistry in my body:
My manners are tearing off heads—

The allotment of death.
For the one path of my flight is direct
Through the bones of the living.
No arguments assert my right:

The sun is behind me.
Nothing has changed since I began.
My eye has permitted no change.
I am going to keep things like this.

TED HUGHES

A POISON TREE

I was angry with my friend :
I told my wrath, my wrath did end.
I was angry with my foe :
I told it not, my wrath did grow.

And I water'd it in fears,
Night and morning with my tears;
And I sunned it with smiles,
And with soft deceitful wiles.

And it grew both day and night,
Till it bore an apple bright;
And my foe beheld it shine,
And he knew that it was mine,

And into my garden stole
When the night had veil'd the pole :
In the morning glad I see
My foe outstretch'd beneath the tree.

WILLIAM BLAKE

FIGHTING FRENZY

I sleep until the beginning of the last night watch;
I hear a woman asking to speak with me;
She tells me news that kills my soul.
I take my saddle by the pommel and girths,
I grasp the handle of my shield where it is fixed in it,
I make it vibrate to the point of splitting,
It gives an even, long-drawn sound, like the
    sounds that are sometimes heard high in the air,
I feel the vibration echo in all my bones,
I draw my shield lightly along my leg.

EBBEKI AG BOUKEN
North Africa

WOMAN'S SONG OF CORN GROWING

Footprints I make! I go to the field with eager haste.
Footprints I make! Amid rustling leaves I stand.
Footprints I make! Amid yellow blossoms I stand.
Footprints I make! I stand with exultant pride.
Footprints I make! I hasten homeward with a
    burden of gladness.
Footprints I make! There's joy and gladness in
    my home.
Footprints I make! I stand amidst a day of
    contentment!

North American Indians

90

TRANSPLANTING

Watching hands transplanting,
Turning and tamping,
Lifting the young plants with two fingers,
Sifting in a palm-full of fresh loam,—
One swift movement,—
Then plumping in the bunched roots,
A single twist of the thumbs, a tamping and
    turning,
All in one,
Quick on the wooden bench,
A shaking down, while the stem stays straight,
Once, twice, and a faint third thump,—
Into the flat-box it goes,
Ready for the long days under the sloped glass:

The sun warming the fine loam,
The young horns winding and unwinding,
Creaking their thin spines,
The underleaves, the smallest buds
Breaking into nakedness,
The blossoms extending
Out into the sweet air,
The whole flower extending outward,
Stretching and reaching.

THEODORE ROETHKE

91

MY DAD'S THUMB

My dad's thumb
can stick pins in wood
without flinching—
it can crush family-size matchboxes
in one stroke
and lever off jam-jar lids without piercing
at the pierce here sign.

If it wanted
it could be a bath-plug
or a paint-scraper
a keyhole cover or a tap-tightener.

It's already a great nutcracker
and if it dressed up
it could easily pass
as a broad bean or a big toe.

In actual fact, it's quite simply
the world's fastest envelope burster.

MICHAEL ROSEN

THE PICNIC IN JAMMU

Uncle Ayub swung me round and round
till the horizon became a rail
banked high upon the Himalayas.
The trees signalled me past. I whistled,
shut my eyes through tunnels of the air.
The family laughed, watching me puff
out my muscles, healthily aggressive.

This was late summer, before the snows
come to Kashmir, this was picnic time.

Then, uncoupling me from the sky, he
plunged me into the river, himself
a bough with me dangling at its end.
I went purple as a plum. He reared
back and lowered the branch of his arm
to grandma who swallowed me with a kiss.
Laughter peeled away my goosepimples.

This was late summer, before the snows
come to Kashmir, this was picnic time.

After we'd eaten, he aimed grapes at
my mouth. I flung at him the shells of
pomegranates and ran off. He tracked
me down the river-bank. We battled,
melon-rind and apple-core our arms.
'You two!' grandma cried. 'Stop fighting, you'll
tire yourselves to death!' We didn't listen.

This was late summer, before the snows
come to Kashmir and end children's games.

ZULFIKAR GHOSE

JAMAICAN FISHERMAN

Across the sand I saw a black man stride
To fetch his fishing gear and broken things,
And silently that splendid body cried
Its proud descent from ancient chiefs and kings,
Across the sand I saw him naked stride;
Sang his black body in the sun's white light
The velvet coolness of dark forests wide,
The blackness of the jungle's starless night.
He stood beside the old canoe which lay
Upon the beach; swept up within his arms
The broken nets and careless lounged away
Towards his hut beneath the ragged palms . . .
Nor knew how fiercely spoke his body then
Of ancient wealth and freeborn regal men.

PHILIP M. SHERLOCK

THE LAMENT OF THE BANANA MAN

Gal, I'm tellin' you, I'm tired fo' true,
Tired of Englan', tired o' you.
But I can' go back to Jamaica now. . . .

I'm here in Englan', I'm drawin' pay,
I go to de underground every day—
Eight hours is all, half-hour fo' lunch,
M' uniform's free, an' m' ticket punch—
Punchin' tickets not hard to do,
When I'm tired o' punchin', I let dem through.

I get a paid holiday once a year.
Ol' age an' sickness can' touch me here.

I have a room o' m' own, an' a iron bed,
Dunlopillo under m' head,
A Morphy-Richards to warm de air,
A formica table, an easy chair.
I have summer clothes, an' winter clothes,
An' paper kerchiefs to blow m' nose.

My yoke is easy, my burden is light,
I know a place I can go to, any night.
Dis place Englan'! I'm not complainin',
If it col', it col', if it rainin', it rainin'.
I don' min' if it's mostly night,
Dere's always inside, or de sodium light.

I don' min' white people starin' at me
Dey don' want me here? Don't is deir country?
You won' catch me bawlin' any homesick tears
If I don' see Jamaica for a t'ousand years!

. . . Gal, I'm tellin' you, I'm tired fo' true,
Tired of Englan', tired o' you,
I can' go back to Jamaica now—
But I'd want to die there, anyhow.

EVAN JONES

THE PARK

In the middle of the city
Is an open space called a Park;
It is difficult for us to do what we like there
Even after dark.

In the middle of the Park there is a statue,
A huge man made of stone;
We are not allowed to climb his legs or scribble on
   his trousers,
He has to be left alone.

In the middle of the grass there is some water
Surrounded by an asphalt path;
We are forbidden to fish or throw stones into it
Or swim or take a bath.

In the middle of the water is an island
Full of mysterious things,
But none of us has ever set foot upon it
Because none of us has wings.

OLIVE DEHN

GRANDFATHER

I remember
His sparse white hair and lean face . . .
Creased eyes that twinkled when he laughed
And the sea-worn skin
Patterned to a latticework of lines.
I remember
His blue-veined, calloused hands,
Long gnarled fingers
Stretching out towards the fire—
Three fingers missing—
Yet he was able to make model yachts
And weave baskets.
Each bronzed Autumn
He would gather berries.
Each breathing Spring
His hands were filled with flowers.
I remember
Worshipping his fisherman's yarns,
Watching his absorbed expression
As he solved the daily crossword
With the slim cigarette, hand rolled,
Placed between his lips.
I remember
The snowdrops,
The impersonal hospital bed,
The reek of antiseptic.

I remember, too,
The weeping child
And wilting daffodils
Laid upon his grave.

SUSAN HRYNKOW
aged 13

THE COWBOY'S LAMENT

As I walked out in the streets of Laredo,
As I walked out in Laredo one day,
I spied a poor cowboy wrapped up in white linen,
Wrapped up in white linen as cold as the clay.

Oh beat the drum slowly and play the fife lowly,
Play the Dead March as you carry me along;
Take me to the green valley, there lay the sod
   o'er me,
For I'm a young cowboy and I know I've done
   wrong.

I see by your outfit that you are a cowboy—
These words he did say as I boldly stepped by.
Come sit down beside me and hear my sad story,
I am shot in the breast and I know I must die.

Let sixteen gamblers come handle my coffin,
Let sixteen cowboys come sing me a song.
Take me to the graveyard and lay the sod o'er me,
For I'm a poor cowboy and I know I've done
   wrong.

My friends and relations they live in the Nation,
They know not where their boy has gone.
I first came to Texas and hired to a ranchman.
Oh I'm a young cowboy and I know I've done
   wrong.

It was once in the saddle I used to go dashing,
It was once in the saddle I used to go gay
First to the dram-house and then to the
   card-house,
Got shot in the breast and I am dying to-day.

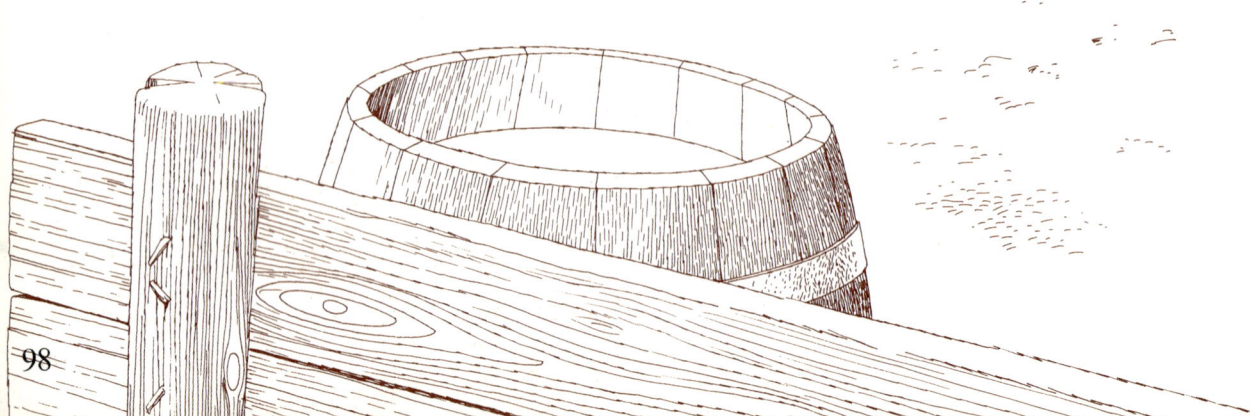

Get six jolly cowboys to carry my coffin,
Get six pretty maidens to bear up my pall.
Put bunches of roses all over my coffin,
Put roses to deaden the sods as they fall.

Then swing your rope slowly and rattle your
    spurs lowly,
And give a wild whoop as you carry me along,
And in the grave throw me and roll the sod
    o'er me,
For I'm a young cowboy and I know I've
    done wrong.

Oh bury beside me my knife and six-shooter,
My spurs on my heel, as you sing me a song,
And over my coffin put a bottle of brandy
That the cowboys may drink as they carry me
    along.

Go bring me a cup, a cup of cold water
To cool my parched lips, the cowboy then said;
Before I returned his soul had departed,
And gone to the round-up, the cowboy was dead.

We beat the drum slowly and played the fife lowly,
And bitterly wept as we bore him along;
For we all loved our comrade, so brave, young,
    and handsome,
We all loved our comrade although he'd
    done wrong.

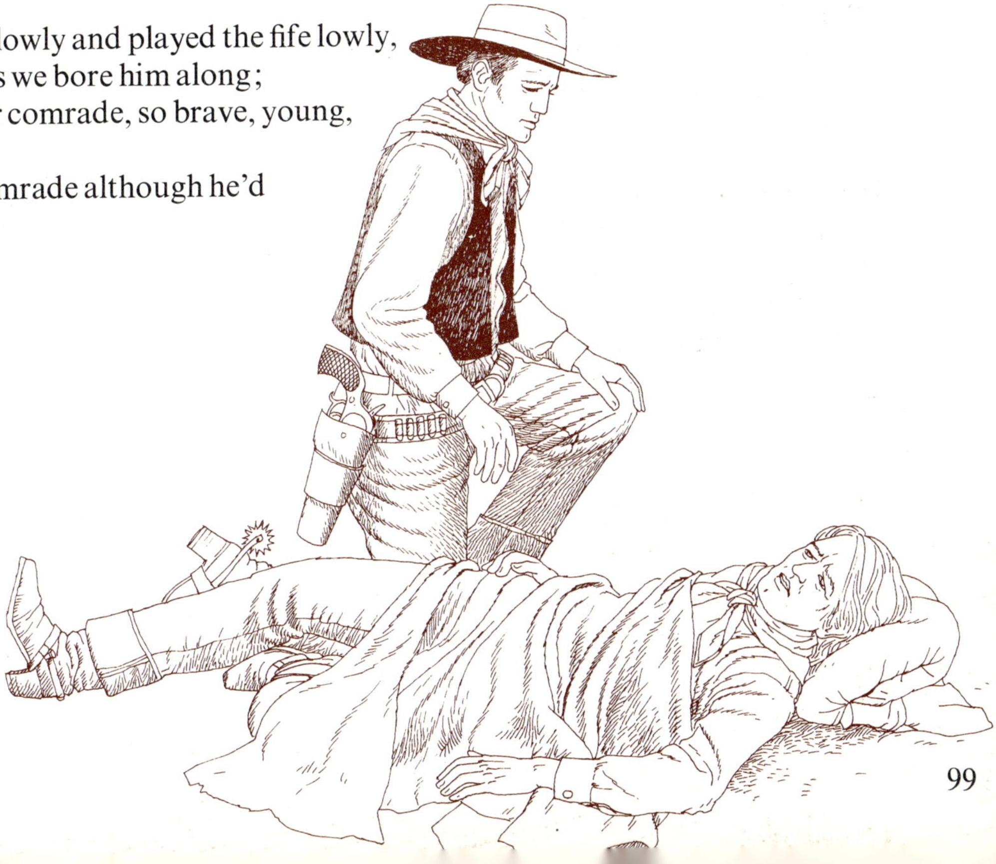

THE LYKE-WAKE DIRGE

This same night, this same night,
　　Every night and all,
Fire and fleet and candle-light,
　　And Christ receive thy soul.

When thou from hence doest pass away,
　　Every night and all,
To Whinny-moor thou come at last,
　　And Christ receive thy soul.

If ever thou gave either stockings or shoes,
　　Every night and all,
Sit thee down and put them on,
　　And Christ receive thy soul.

But if stockings or shoes thou never gave none,
　　Every night and all,
The whinnies[1] shall prick thee to the bare bone,
　　And Christ receive thy soul.

From Whinny-moor that thou may pass,
　　Every night and all,
To Bridge of Dread thou come at last,
　　And Christ receive thy soul.

From Bridge of Dead that thou may pass
　　Every night and all,
To Purgatory fire thou come at last,
　　And Christ receive thy soul.

If ever thou gave either milk or drink,
　　Every night and all,
The fire shall never make thee shrink,
　　And Christ receive thy soul.

But if milk nor drink thou never gave none,
　　Every night and all,
The fire shall burn thee to the bare bone,
　　And Christ receive thy soul.

This same night, this same night,
　　Every night and all,
Fire and fleet and candle-light,
　　And Christ receive thy soul.

[1] Whinnies are gorse.

A LAND DIRGE

Call for the robin-redbreast and the wren,
Since o'er shady groves they hover,
And with leaves and flowers do cover
The friendless bodies of unburied men.
Call unto his funeral dole
The ant, the field-mouse, and the mole,
To rear him hillocks that shall keep him warm,
And (when gay tombs are robbed) sustain
    no harm;
But keep the wolf far thence, that's foe to men,
For with his nails he'll dig them up again.

JOHN WEBSTER

AS IT WAS

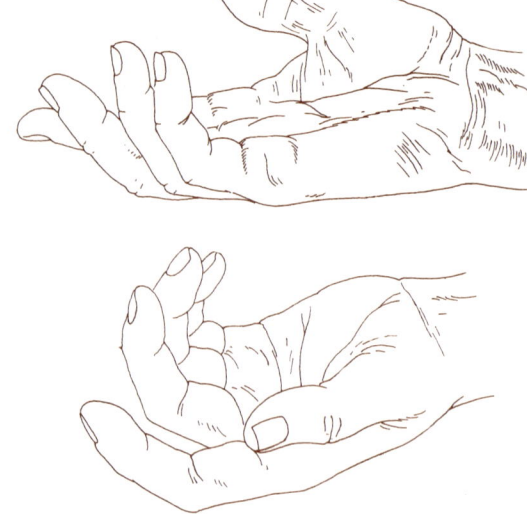

It did not seem important at the time:
We gave them pity when they wanted gold,
We could not help it: we were never told.

We'd lost our glasses, so we could not see:
We went home early from the Pantomime—
It did not seem important at the time.

We walked away: it was not our concern.
No doubt there was some fruit upon the Tree:
We'd lost our glasses, so we could not see.

We could not help it: we were never told.
We heard a shot: the guards looked very stern.
We walked away: it was not our concern.

We could not help it: we were never told.
No doubt there were some rumours of a crime,
We'd lost our glasses, so we could not see.
We walked away: it was not our concern.
The streets were dark and it was very cold.
It did not seem important at the time.

JOHN MANDER

AT THE RAILWAY STATION, UPWAY

'There is not much that I can do,
     For I've no money that's quite my own!'
     Spoke up the pitying child—
A little boy with a violin
At the station before the train came in,—
'But I can play my fiddle to you,
And a nice one 'tis, and good in tone!'

     The man in the handcuffs smiled;
The constable looked, and he smiled, too,
     As the fiddle began to twang;
And the man in the handcuffs suddenly sang
          With grimful glee:
          'This life so free
          Is the thing for me!'
And the constable smiled, and said no word,
As if unconscious of what he heard;
And so they went on till the train came in—
The convict, and boy with the violin.

THOMAS HARDY

103

THE FIDDLER OF DOONEY

When I play on my fiddle in Dooney,
Folk dance like a wave of the sea ;
My cousin is priest in Kilvarnet,
My brother in Mocharabuiee.[1]

I passed my brother and cousin :
They read in their books of prayer ;
I read in my book of songs
I bought at the Sligo fair.

When we come at the end of time
To Peter sitting in state,
He will smile on the three old spirits,
But call me first through the gate ;

For the good are always the merry,
Save by an evil chance,
And the merry love the fiddle,
And the merry love to dance :

And when the folk there spy me,
They will all come up to me,
With 'Here is the fiddler of Dooney !'
And dance like a wave of the sea.

W. B. YEATS

[1] Pronounced as if spelt 'Mockrabwee'.

Magic and Mystery

About the poems

Poetry and magic have always been closely linked. Some of the earliest poems of all were charms and magic spells. Words with a rhythm or rhyme are much easier to remember, so important pieces of knowledge were often passed on in that way.

People remembered **Charms** against things that came mysteriously, like burns or hiccups.

The fact that they were in rhyme and had a rhythm gave them a sort of power. They seemed to *mean* more, because the rhymes held unexpected things together.

Other verses give magic to ordinary life by suggesting that days of the week, or colours, have a meaning of their own. The fishermen enjoy the thought of coming home for the weekend and make a rhyme about the different days. Can you make a rhyme like that about the days of the school week?

Warts are another of the mysterious things that happen to our bodies. They are harmless, but nobody likes having them and the poem **Warts** tells us about ways in which people try to make them go away.

There is always something magical about having knowledge that other people don't have, and also about getting hold of it. That is why we all enjoy riddles.

The **Riddles** given here are from *The Hobbit* by J. R. R. Tolkien, and are about things that are still important to us. Can you solve them? The illustration next to each one will give you a clue to the answer. In *The Hobbit* the riddles are part of a life-or-death contest, where the one who fails to answer the other's riddle will fall into his power.

In **The False Knight upon the Road** much the same is happening. The small boy on his way to school meets a knight who tries to frighten him with threatening questions, but each time the boy has a good answer ready—just as the rider has in **O where are you going?**

The next poem, **I saw a Peacock**, is one long riddle: does it take any of the magic away when you know the answer? There are no answers to the riddles in **Ariel Sings**—does this make it more magical?

Although magic often goes with power, Ben Jonson's poem **It is not Growing like a Tree** is a reminder that small and perfect things can sometimes be the most magical.

Now read **Kubla Khan** aloud in a slow, chanting voice. See how this gives the poem a sense of power and mystery. Try drawing the scene in the poem and then ask your friends to do the same. You will find how many ways there are of seeing it, and how there is no 'right' one.

Sometimes wonder comes from seeing something unexpectedly, or in an unusual light. Imagine yourself as the Indian in **The Discovery**. Or think how it would be to come into **Nottamun Town**. Why do you think the riddles at the end of this poem are so very difficult?

So long as our imaginations are alive, there is always some magic in the world. Listen to the wind from your bedroom and you will know what Robert Louis Stevenson means in **Windy Nights**. And although none of us has ever experienced what happens in **Unwelcome**, we all know what it would be like.

Reading Wallace Stevens' poem **Ploughing on Sunday** after **Unwelcome** is rather like waking up after a bad dream and seeing how beautiful the world is after all. Many poets would not use some of the words he uses, like 'Tum-ti-tum', for fear of sounding childish, but Stevens knows that some things feel magically the same whether you are a small child or a grown-up. T.E. Hulme, in **Autumn**, too, knows that magic is always present in our lives. Does is make the stars seem ordinary to say that they are like town children, or more magical? What does it do to the moon to say it is like a forgotten balloon?

The moon is often associated with magic, partly because of its strange light and partly because of its mysterious effect on the natural world—especially the sea. People tell stories about it; they picture a moon-goddess, or 'the man in the moon'; or, like the Japanese poet who wrote **The Hare in the Moon**, they see a hare and imagine how it got there.

Judith Wright in **Full Moon Rhyme** turns this idea around, by making all the dogs who howl at the moon do so because they too see a hare in it; and in **Moon-Wind** Ted Hughes paints a strange and rather eerie picture of the kind of wind you might find on the moon.

A feeling of strangeness can come from doing something quite ordinary like climbing a hill, and seeing how small the world suddenly looks (**High on the Hill**). Or from imagining countries we have never been to, as Robert Louis Stevenson does in **Travel**.

But when you actually go to a strange country you may still have a feeling that the magic is a little further on—like the American in another state who imagines that the true place to be is **Idaho**.

Two of the last poems are 'chain poems' in which everything connects to something else until you end up with some quite unexpected connection.

The Indians of **Aztec Song** might not find this as surprising as we do, because they feel closer to the earth than modern man does.

There's something more like a detective story in **This is the Key**, where we half expect to find at the end that we have discovered the key to a mystery. The key we find, however, is the same one that the Aztec Indians know: it is a key to life itself.

The boy in **Is this all?** on the other hand cannot find any mystery or excitement in his life. Do you sympathize with him? Any why do you think his mother smiles?

There is just a touch of the sinister about the last poem, but there is a good deal more of delight. Imagine a Christmas morning on which you never got to the end of unwrapping your presents. **Warning to Children** has something of the same magic, and it also helps to explain why all of us enjoy poems that have some sort of mystery about them—and how good poetry can be at expressing that mystery.

RIDDLES

Voiceless it cries,
Wingless flutters,
Toothless bites,
Mouthless mutters.

What has roots as nobody sees,
Is taller than trees
   Up, up it goes,
    And yet never grows?

It cannot be seen, cannot be felt,
Cannot be heard, cannot be smelt.
It lies behind stars and under hills,
   And empty holes it fills.
It comes first and follows after,
   Ends life, kills laughter.

Alive without breath,
As cold as death;
Never thirsty, ever drinking,
All in mail never clinking.

Thirty white horses on a red hill,
    First they champ,
    Then they stamp,
Then they stand still.

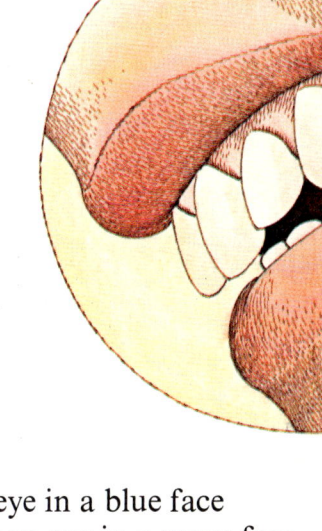

An eye in a blue face
Saw an eye in a green face.
'That eye is like to this eye'
Said the first eye,
'But in low place
Not in high place.'

A box without hinges, key, or lid,
Yet golden treasure inside is hid.

This thing all things devours:
Birds, beasts, trees, flowers;
Gnaws iron, bites steel;
Grinds hard stones to meal;
Slays king, ruins town,
And beats high mountain down.

J. R. R. TOLKIEN

CHARMS

Hickup, hickup, go away,
Come again another day:
Hickup, hickup, when I bake,
I'll give to you a butter-cake.

Blue is true,
Yellow's jealous,
Green's forsaken,
Red's brazen,
White is love,
And black is death!

Cut them on Monday, you cut them for health;
Cut them on Tuesday, you cut them for wealth;
Cut them on Wednesday, you cut them for news;
Cut them on Thursday, a new pair of shoes;
Cut them on Friday, you cut them for sorrow;
Cut them on Saturday, see your true love
  tomorrow;
Cut them on Sunday, the devil will be with you
  all the week.

Two angels from the north,
One brought fire, the other brought frost:
    Out fire!
    In frost!
In the name of the Father, Son, and Holy Ghost.

Today is silver Saturday,
The morn's the resting day,
Monday up and to it again,
And Tuesday, push away.

WARTS

You can sell them for a penny to
your mother

                    or

You can tie knots for each one
in a piece of string
and plant it at the bottom of your garden
and water it
every morning
that makes them grow under the earth

                    or

You can have them charmed
if you know a charmer
there are lots in Cornwall you must
leave her a gift and not say thankyou
then she will sing
an incantation

                    or

there is the witches way.
You take a special white round stone
for every one
and put them in a pretty red bag
throw it over your shoulder
into the middle of the road—

*Don't touch that bag it's got
warts in it*

                    or

If you can find the green toad you
got them from you can
give them back to him if he'll have them

                    or

You can rub snails on them or slugs
and if that doesn't cure them

you still want them

JENI COUZYN
'The Soul is the Breath in your Body'

THE FALSE KNIGHT UPON
THE ROAD

'O where are you going?'
Quoth the false knight upon the road:
'I'm going to school.'
Quoth the wee boy, and still he stood.

'What is that upon your back?'
Quoth the false knight upon the road:
'Why, sure it is my books.'
Quoth the wee boy, and still he stood.

'What is that you've got in your arm?'
Quoth the false knight upon the road:
'Why sure it is my peat.'[1]
Quoth the wee boy, and still he stood.

'Whose are those sheep?'
Quoth the false knight upon the road:
'They're mine and my mother's.'
Quoth the wee boy, and still he stood.

'How many of them are mine?'
Quoth the false knight upon the road:
'All them that have blue tails.'
Quoth the wee boy, and still he stood.

'I wish you were on yon tree.'
Quoth the false knight upon the road:
'And a good ladder under me.'
Quoth the wee boy, and still he stood.

'And the ladder for to break.'
Quoth the false knight upon the road:
'And *you* for to fall down.'
Quoth the wee boy, and still he stood.

'I wish you were in yon sea.'
Quoth the false knight upon the road:
'And a good boat under me.'
Quoth the wee boy, and still he stood,

'And the boat for to break.'
Quoth the false knight on the road:
'And *you* to be drowned.'
Quoth the wee boy, and still he stood.

112

[1] Peat for the school fire.

'O WHERE ARE YOU GOING?'

'O where are you going?' said reader to rider,
'That valley is fatal when furnaces burn,
Yonder's the midden whose odours will madden,
That gap is the grave where the tall return.'

'O do you imagine,' said fearer to farer,
'That dusk will delay on your path to the pass,
Your diligent looking discover the lacking
Your footsteps feel from granite to grass?'

'O what was that bird,' said horror to hearer,
'Did you see that shape in the twisted trees?
Behind you swiftly the figure comes softly,
The spot on your skin is a shocking disease.'

'Out of this house'—said rider to reader,
'Yours never will'—said farer to fearer,
'They're looking for you'—said hearer to horror,
As he left them there, as he left them there.

W. H. AUDEN

I SAW A PEACOCK WITH A FIERY TAIL

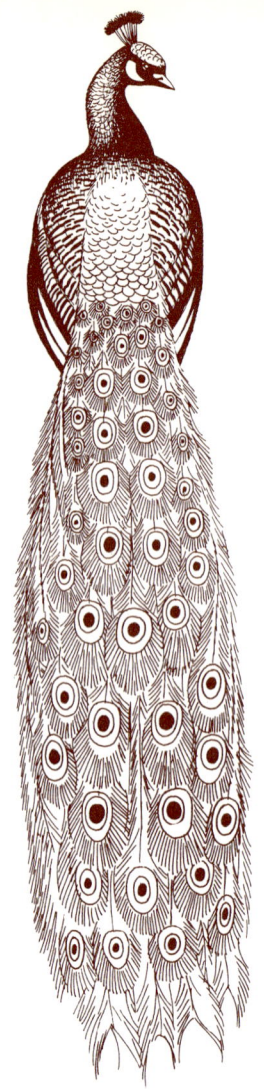

I saw a Peacock with a fiery tail,
I saw a blazing Comet drop down hail,
I saw a Cloud with ivy circled round,
I saw a sturdy Oak creep on the ground,
I saw a Pismire swallow up a whale,
I saw a raging Sea brim full of ale,
I saw a Venice Glass sixteen foot deep,
I saw a Well full of men's tears that weep,
I saw their Eyes all in a flame of fire,
I saw a House as big as the moon and higher,
I saw the Sun even in the midst of night,
I saw the Man that saw this wondrous sight.

(To solve the riddle, read from the middle of the first line to the middle of the next, and so on through the poem)

ARIEL SINGS

Full fathom five thy father lies;
  Of his bones are coral made;
Those are pearls that were his eyes:
  Nothing of him that doth fade,
But doth suffer a sea-change
Into something rich and strange.
Sea-nymphs hourly ring his knell:
    (*Chorus:*) Ding-dong bell.

WILLIAM SHAKESPEARE
The Tempest

IT IS NOT GROWING LIKE A TREE . . .

It is not growing like a tree
In bulk, doth make man better be;
Or standing long an oak, three hundred year,
To fall a log at last, dry, bald, and sere:
A lily of a day
Is fairer far, in May,
Although it fall and die that night;
It was the plant and flower of light.
In small proportions we just beauty see,
And in short measures life may perfect be.

BEN JONSON

THE DISCOVERY

There was an Indian, who had known no change,
   Who strayed content along a sunlit beach
Gathering shells. He heard a sudden strange
   Commingled noise; looked up; and gasped
     for speech.
For in the bay, where nothing was before,
   Moved on the sea, by magic, huge canoes,
With bellying cloths on poles, and not one oar,
   And fluttering coloured signs and clambering
     crews.

And he, in fear, this naked man alone,
   His fallen hands forgetting all their shells,
His lips gone pale, knelt low behind a stone,
   And stared, and saw, and did not understand,
Columbus's doom-burdened caravels
   Slant to the shore, and all their seamen land.

                J. C. SQUIRE

NOTTAMUN TOWN

In Nottamun Town not a soul would look up,
Not a soul would look up, not a soul would
   look down,
Not a soul would look up, not a soul would
   look down
To tell me the way to Nottamun Town.

I rode a big horse that was called a grey mare,
Grey mane and tail, grey stripes down his back,
Grey mane and tail, grey stripes down his back,
There weren't a hair on him but what was
   called black.

She stood so still, she threw me to the dirt,
She tore my hide and bruised my shirt;
From stirrup to stirrup, I mounted again
And on my ten toes I rode over the plain.

Met the King and the Queen and a company
   of men
A-walking behind and a-riding before.
A stark naked drummer came walking along
With his hands in his bosom a-beating his drum.

Sat down on a hot and cold frozen stone
Ten thousand stood round me and I was alone.
Took my heart in my hand to keep my head warm.
Ten thousand got drowned that never were born.

KUBLA KHAN

In Xanadu did Kubla Khan
A stately pleasure-dome decree:
Where Alph, the sacred river, ran
Through caverns measureless to man
   Down to a sunless sea.
So twice five miles of fertile ground
With walls and towers were girdled round:
And here were gardens bright with sinuous rills,
Where blossomed many an incense-bearing tree;
And here were forests ancient as the hills,
Enfolding sunny spots of greenery.

But oh! that deep romantic chasm which slanted
Down the green hill athwart a cedarn cover!
A savage place! as holy and enchanted
As e'er beneath a waning moon was haunted
By woman wailing for her demon-lover!
And from this chasm, with ceaseless turmoil
   seething,
As if this earth in fast thick pants were breathing,
A mighty fountain momently was forced:
Amid whose swift half-intermitted burst
Huge fragments vaulted like rebounding hail,
Or chaffy grain beneath the thresher's flail:
And 'mid these dancing rocks at once and ever
It flung up momently the sacred river.
Five miles meandering with a mazy motion
Through wood and dale the sacred river ran,
Then reached the caverns measureless to man,
And sank in tumult to a lifeless ocean:
And 'mid this tumult Kubla heard from far
Ancestral voices prophesying war!

   The shadow of the dome of pleasure
   Floated midway on the waves;
   Where was heard the mingled measure
   From the fountain and the caves.
It was a miracle of rare device,
A sunny pleasure-dome with caves of ice!

   A damsel with a dulcimer
   In a vision once I saw:
   It was an Abyssinian maid,

And on her dulcimer she played,
Singing of Mount Abora.
Could I revive within me
Her symphony and song,
To such a deep delight 'twould win me,
That with music loud and long,
I would build that dome in air,
That sunny dome! those caves of ice!
And all who heard should see them there,
And all should cry, Beware! Beware!
His flashing eyes, his floating hair!
Weave a circle round him thrice,
And close your eyes with holy dread,
For he on honey-dew hath fed,
And drunk the milk of Paradise.

S. T. COLERIDGE

WINDY NIGHTS

Whenever the moon and stars are set,
  Whenever the wind is high,
All night long in the dark and wet,
  A man goes riding by.
Late in the night when the fires are out,
Why does he gallop and gallop about?

Whenever the trees are crying aloud,
  And ships are tossed at sea,
By, on the highway, low and loud,
  By at the gallop goes he.
By at the gallop he goes, and then
By he comes back at the gallop again.

ROBERT LOUIS STEVENSON

120

UNWELCOME

We were young, we were merry, we were very very wise,
    And the door stood open at our feast,
When there passed us a woman with the West in her eyes,
    And a man with his back to the East.

O, still grew the hearts that were beating so fast,
    The loudest voice was still.
The jest died away on our lips as they passed,
    And the rays of July struck chill.

The cups of red wine turned pale on the board,
    The white bread black as soot.
The hound forgot the hand of her lord,
    She fell down at his foot.

Low let me die, where the dead dog lies,
    Ere I sit me down again at a feast,
When there passes a woman with the West in her eyes,
    And a man with his back to the East.

MARY COLERIDGE

PLOUGHING ON SUNDAY

The white cock's tail
Tosses in the wind.
The turkey-cock's tail
Glitters in the sun.

Water in the fields.
The wind pours down.
The feathers flare
And bluster in the wind.

Remus, blow your horn!
I'm ploughing on Sunday,
Ploughing North America.
Blow your horn!

Tum-ti-tum,
Ti-tum-tum-tum!
The turkey-cock's tail
Spreads to the sun.

The white cock's tail
Streams to the moon.
Water in the fields.
The wind pours down.

WALLACE STEVENS

ABOVE THE DOCK

Above the quiet dock in midnight,
Tangled in the tall mast's corded height,
Hangs the moon. What seemed so far away
Is but a child's balloon, forgotten after play.

T. E. HULME

AUTUMN

A touch of cold in the Autumn night—
I walked abroad,
And saw the ruddy moon lean over a hedge
Like a red-faced farmer.
I did not stop to speak, but nodded,
And round about were the wistful stars
With white faces like town children.

T. E. HULME

FULL MOON RHYME

There's a hare in the moon tonight,
crouching alone in the bright
buttercup field of the moon;
and all the dogs in the world
howl at the hare in the moon.

'I chased that hare to the sky,'
the hungry dogs all cry.
'The hare jumped into the moon
and left me here in the cold.
I chased that hare to the moon.'

'Come down again, wild hare.
We can see you there,'
the dogs all howl to the moon.
'Come down again to the world,
you mad black hare in the moon,

'or we will grow wings and fly
up to the star-grassed sky
to hunt you out of the moon,'
the hungry dogs of the world
howl at the hare in the moon.

JUDITH WRIGHT

THE HARE IN THE MOON

Long long ago, they say,
Lived a monkey, a hare, and a fox.
Together they formed a bond
Of friendship:
In the day, they romped
In the hills and fields,
At night, to their
Forest they returned.
And so time passed,
Until the god who lives
In the eternal heavens
Heard the story.
'But is it true?'
He asked, and turned himself
Into an old man,
Teetering along to see.
There he found them
Just as he had heard,
Romping and playing,
Their hearts made one.
Resting his limbs awhile,
Pausing to get his breath,
He threw away his staff
And shouted, 'Help me!
Help a hungry old man!'
'That's not hard,' they said,
And then, quick as a flash,
From the copse behind
The monkey gathered berries;
From the river bank in front
The fox snapped up a fish;
But the hare, hopping
All about the place,
Did not a thing to help.
'Oh! that hare—his idea's
Always different,' they cursed.
But all to no good. Then,
'Break these twigs,' said monkey,
'Light a fire,' said fox.
Hare did as he was told.
And then, into the smoke
And flames they hurled him,
And served him up to
The old man, all unwitting.

He, lifting his eyes
To the heavens that last for ever,
Sobbed and wept and then
Rolled prostrate on the ground.
Soon, beating on his breast,
He asked, 'Which of the three,
These three old friends, which
Treated me the best?
They were all kind.' And yet,
Thinking that the hare
Was the finest of them all,
He took him, dead,
And cast him high up
To the palace of the moon
In the heavens that last for ever.

RYŌKAN

THE WITCHES' CHARM

The owl is abroad, the bat and the toad,
　　And so is the cat-o'-mountain;
The ant and the mole sit both in a hole,
　　And frog peeps out o' the fountain;
The dogs they do bay, and the timbrels play,
　　The spindle is now a-turning;
The moon it is red, and the stars are fled,
　　But all the sky is a-burning:
The ditch is made, and our nails the spade,
With pictures full, of wax and of wool;
Their livers I stick with needles quick:
That lacks but the blood, to make up the flood.
　　Quickly, dame, then, bring your part in,
　　Spur, spur upon little Martin,
　　Merrily, merrily, make him sail,
　　A worm in his mouth, and a thorn in's tail,
　　Fire above and fire below,
　　With a whip i' your hand to make him go.
　　Oh, now she's come!
　　Let all be dumb.

BEN JONSON

126

MOON-WIND

There is no wind on the moon at all
    Yet things get blown about.
In utter utter stillness
    Your candle shivers out.

In utter stillness
    A giant marquee
Booms and flounders past you
    Like a swan at sea.

In utter utter stillness
    While you stand in the street
A squall of hens and cabbages
    Knocks you off your feet.

In utter utter stillness
    While you stand agog
A tearing twisting sheet of pond
    Clouts you with a frog.

A camp of caravans suddenly
    Squawks and takes off.
A ferris wheel bounds along the skyline
    Like a somersaulting giraffe.

Roots and foundations, nails and screws,
    Nothing can hold fast,
Nothing can resist the moon's
    Dead-still blast.

TED HUGHES

127

TRAVEL

I should like to rise and go
Where the golden apples grow;
Where below another sky
Parrot islands anchored lie,
And, watched by cockatoos and goats,
Lonely Crusoes building boats;
Where in sunshine reaching out
Eastern cities, miles about,
Are with mosque and minaret
Among sandy gardens set,
And the rich goods from near and far
Hang for sale in the bazaar;
Where the Great Wall round China goes,
And on one side the desert blows,
And with bell and voice and drum,
Cities on the other hum;
Where are forests, hot as fire,
Wide as England, tall as a spire,
Full of apes and coconuts
And the negro hunters' huts;
Where the knotty crocodile
Lies and blinks in the Nile,
And the red flamingo flies
Hunting fish before his eyes;

Where in jungles, near and far,
Man-devouring tigers are,
Lying close and giving ear
Lest the hunt be drawing near,
Or a comer-by be seen
Swinging in a palanquin;
Where among the desert sands
Some deserted city stands,
All its children, sweep and prince,
Grown to manhood ages since,
Not a foot in street or house,
Not a stir of child or mouse,
And when kindly falls the night,
In all the town no spark of light.
There I'll come when I'm a man
With a camel caravan;
Light a fire in the gloom
Of some dusty dining-room;
See the pictures on the walls,
Heroes, fights and festivals;
And in a corner find the toys
Of the old Egyptian boys.

ROBERT LOUIS STEVENSON

HIGH ON THE HILL

High on the hill I can see it all,
the anthill men and the doll's house town,
the bowl of sea and the trim toy ships.
Here only the trees at hand are tall.

High on the hill I can touch a cloud
or measure miles with my fingertips,
can hide the town with a palm turned down
and drown its noise when I speak aloud.

High on the hill it's all a joke
and I wonder why I bothered at all
with the clockwork cars and the anthill folk
that height and distance make so small.

TOM WRIGHT

THERE WAS A NAUGHTY BOY . . .

There was a naughty Boy,
  And a naughty Boy was he,
He ran away to Scotland
  The people for to see—
    There he found
    That the ground
    Was as hard,
    That a yard
    Was as long,
    That a song
    Was as merry,
    That a cherry
    Was as red—
    That lead
    Was as weighty,
    That fourscore
    Was as eighty,
    That a door
    Was as wooden
    As in England—
    So he stood in
    His shoes
    And he wonder'd,
    He wonder'd,
    He stood in his
    Shoes and he wonder'd . . .

JOHN KEATS

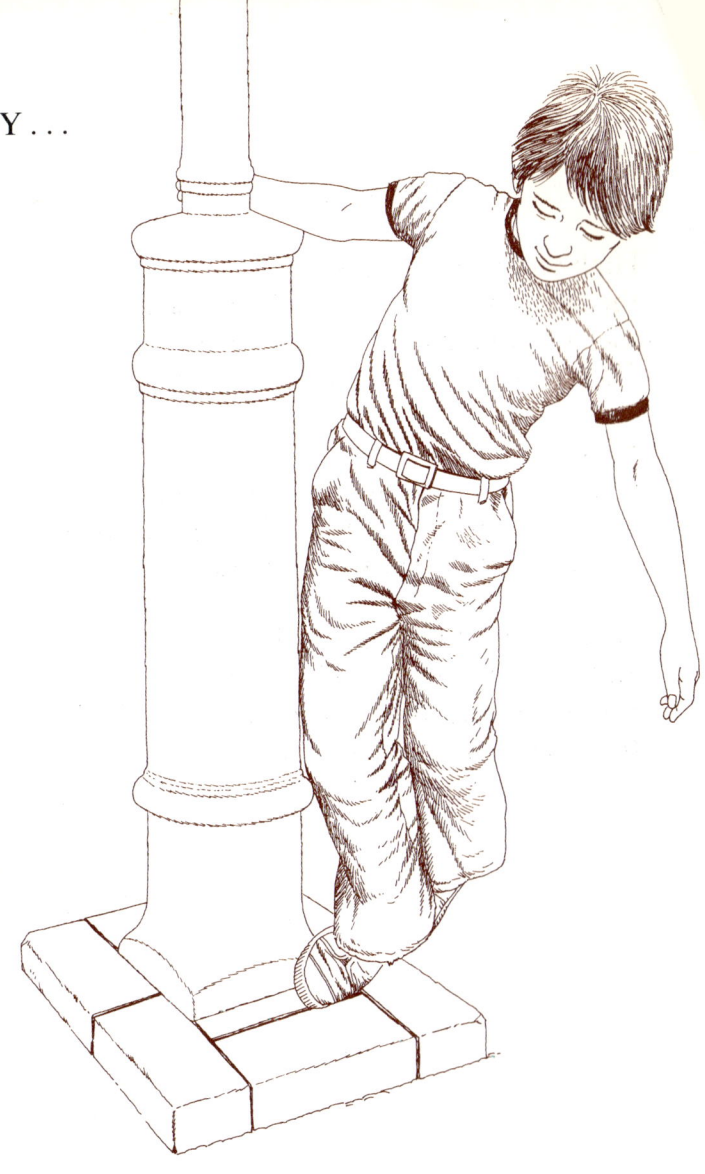

AUNTIE'S SKIRTS

Whenever Auntie moves around,
Her dresses make a curious sound;
They trail behind her up the floor,
And trundle after through the door.

ROBERT LOUIS STEVENSON

IDAHO

They say there is a land
   Where crystal waters flow,
Where veins of purest gold are found
   Way out in Idaho.

We'll need no pick or spade,
   No shovel, pan or hoe,
The largest chunks are on the ground
   Way out in Idaho.

AZTEC SONG

we only came to sleep
we only came to dream
it is not true
no it is not true
that we came to live on the earth

we are changed into the grass of springtime
our hearts will grow green again
and they will open their petals
but our body is like a rose tree
    it puts forth flowers and then withers

Nahuatl Indians, Mexico
translated by LOWELL DUNHAM

THIS IS THE KEY

This is the Key of the Kingdom
In that Kingdom is a city;
In that city is a town;
In that town there is a street;
In that street there winds a lane;
In that lane there is a yard;
In that yard there is a house;
In that house there waits a room;
In that room an empty bed;
And on that bed a basket—
A Basket of Sweet Flowers:
  Of Flowers, of Flowers;
  A Basket of Sweet Flowers.

Flowers in a Basket;
Basket on the bed;
Bed in the chamber;
Chamber in the house;
House in the weedy yard;
Yard in the winding lane;
Lane in the broad street;
Street in the high town;
Town in the city;
City in the Kingdom—
This is the Key of the Kingdom;
  Of the Kingdom this is the Key.

IS THIS ALL?

High on the short-grass hill-top,
By the green and blistered seat,
Mother sat in her blue dress,
And Towser, flopped at her feet.

And near them, hatted and suited,
Father in Sunday sprawl.
Bob asked, 'Is this all the life there is?'
Said Mother, 'Yes, this is all.'

Bob walked across to the hill's edge,
And looked thoughtfully down
At the muddy twist of the river,
At the roofed and castled town.

To climb to this grassy summit
With parents and dog and ball,
Could this be all the life there was?—
Could this be all?

And then to stand and fidget,
Till sharp on the stroke of four
The parents rose and retraced their steps
Down to their own front door;

To a Sunday tea with muffins,
And the Pollards who'd come to call . . .
'Is this all the life there is, Mother?'
Mother smiled. 'This is all.'

JOHN WALSH

WARNING TO CHILDREN

Children, if you dare to think
Of the greatness, rareness, muchness,
Fewness of this precious only
Endless world in which you say
You live, you think of things like this:
Blocks of slate enclosing dappled
Red and green, enclosing tawny
Yellow nets, enclosing white
And black acres of dominoes,
Where a neat brown paper parcel
Tempts you to untie the string.
In the parcel a small island,
On the island a large tree,
On the tree a husky fruit.
Strip the husk and pare the rind off:
In the kernel you will see
Blocks of slate enclosed by dappled
Red and green, enclosed by tawny
Yellow nets, enclosed by white
And black acres of dominoes,
Where the same brown paper parcel—
Children, leave the string alone!
For who dares undo the parcel
Finds himself at once inside it,
On the island, in the fruit,
Blocks of slate about his head,
Finds himself enclosed by dappled
Green and red, enclosed by yellow
Tawny nets, enclosed by black
And white acres of dominoes,
With the same brown paper parcel
Still unopened on his knee.
And, if he then should dare to think
Of the fewness, muchness, rareness,
Greatness of this endless only
Precious world in which he says
He lives—he then unties the string.

ROBERT GRAVES

136

Index of titles and first lines

Index of poets

Acknowledgments

The publishers have made every effort to trace the ownership of all copyrighted material and to secure permission from holders of such poems. They regret any inadvertent error and will be pleased to make the necessary corrections in future printings. Thanks are due to the following:

TELLING A STORY

FABER AND FABER LTD. for 'My Parents Kept me from Children who were Rough' from *Collected Poems* by Stephen Spender, and for 'Surprise' from *Bananas in Pyjamas* by Carey Blyton.

NEW BEACON BOOKS LTD. for 'The Pond' from *The Pond and Other Poems* by Mervyn Morris, © 1973.

GRANADA PUBLISHING LTD. and HARCOURT BRACE JOVANOVICH, INC. for 'maggie and milly and molly and may' from *Complete Poems 1913-1962* by e.e. cummings, © 1956.

MACMILLAN, London and Basingstoke, and MRS HODGSON for 'Stupidity Street' from *Collected Poems* by Ralph Hodgson.

WILLIAM HEINEMANN LTD., LAURENCE POLLINGER LTD. and the Estate of the late MRS. FRIEDA LAWRENCE RAVAGLI for 'Snake' from *The Complete Poems of D.H. Lawrence*.

FRANCES, DAY AND HUNTER LTD. for 'The Rest of the Day's Your Own' by J.P. Long and David Worton, © 1915, and for 'The Lion and Albert' by Marriott Edgar, © 1933.

RAYMOND SOUSTER for 'The Flight of the Rollercoaster'.

ROGER McGOUGH for 'Mad Ad' from *In The Glassroom*.

W.H. ALLEN AND CO. LTD., for 'The Slithergadee' from *Don't Bump the Glump* by Shel Silverstein.

TAKING A CLOSER LOOK

HENRY HOLT AND SONS, New York for 'The Pasture', 'Lodged', 'Stopping by Woods' and 'Neither out Far nor in Deep' from *Collected Poems* by Robert Frost.

MACMILLAN, London and Basingstoke, for 'Madam' from *Jets from Orange* by Zulfikar Ghose, and for 'The Gorilla' (originally entitled 'Au Jardin des Plantes') from *Weep before God* by John Wain.

FABER AND FABER LTD. for 'A March Calf' from *Season Songs* by Ted Hughes and for 'The Lizard' and 'The Waking' from *The Collected Poems of Theodore Roethke*.

OXFORD UNIVERSITY PRESS for 'The Bear' by Frederick Brown from *Every Man Will Shout* edited by Roger Mansfield and Isobel Armstrong, © Oxford University Press 1964, and for 'Hedgehog' from *The Owl in the Tree* by Anthony Thwaite, © Oxford University Press 1963.

ANGUS AND ROBERTSON (Sydney) and the copyright proprietor for 'Weary Will' by A.B. Paterson.

FREDERICK WARNE LTD. for 'Gecko' from *Round About Eight* by Noel Lloyd.

WILLIAM HEINEMANN LTD., LAURENCE POLLINGER LTD. and the Estate of the late MRS FRIEDA LAWRENCE RAVAGLI for 'Sea-weed' and 'Little Fish' from *The Complete Poems of D.H. Lawrence*.

HUTCHINSON PUBLISHING GROUP LTD. for 'Baby Blackbird' from *Young Writers Young Readers* edited by Boris Ford.

JONATHAN CAPE LTD. for 'Snails' by Dominic Hodgkin, © Dominic Hodgkin, 1972, and 'Obituary on the Demolition of a House in Grove Lane, Camberwell' by Maria Dawson, © Maria Dawson, 1972, both from *Fire Words* by Chris Searle.

HARCOURT BRACE JOVANOVITCH, INC. for 'Worms and the Wind' by Carl Sandburg.

THE LITERARY TRUSTEES of Walter de la Mare, and THE SOCIETY OF AUTHORS as their representative, for 'The Fly' from *Collected Rhymes and Verses*.

ROUTLEDGE AND KEGAN PAUL for 'Serious Readers' from *Every Chink of the Ark* by Peter Redgrove, © 1977.

DOBSON BOOKS LTD. for 'Sardines' from *A Book of Milliganimals* by Spike Milligan.

ROBERT GRAVES for 'Lost Love' from Collected Poems, © 1975.

GEORGE G. HARRAP AND CO. LTD., and LITTLE, BROWN AND CO. for 'Snowflakes' from *Mr Bidery's Spidery Garden* by David McCord.

INDIANA UNIVERSITY PRESS for 'After Spending a Night

Alone' by Hsin Ch'i-chi, translated by Irving Yuchang
from *K'uei Hsing*, © 1974.
THE EXECUTORS OF THE W.H. DAVIES ESTATE for 'Leisure'
from *The Complete Poems of W.H. Davies*.

HEROES AND VICTIMS

JONATHAN CAPE LTD. for 'A Hero' (originally entitled
'My Hero') by John Lane, and for 'Another Hero'
(originally entitled 'My Hero') by Anne Marie Hancock,
both from *Fire Words* by Chris Searle.
VICTOR GOLLANCZ LTD. for 'Superman' from *Hoping for a
Hoopoe* by John Updike.
ROGER McGOUGH for 'He Who Owns the Whistle Rules
the World' and 'First Day at School'. both from
In The Glassroom.
DOBSON BOOKS LTD. for 'Hello Mr Python' from *Silly
Verse For Kids* by Spike Milligan.
MRS A.M. WALSH for 'The Bully Asleep' from *The
Roundabout by the Sea* by John Walsh.
ANDRE DEUTSCH LTD. for 'I'm the Big Sleeper' and 'My
Dad's Thumb' from *Mind Your Own Business* by
Michael Rosen.
FABER AND FABER LTD. for 'Hawk Roosting' from *Lupercal*
by Ted Hughes, and for 'Transplanting' from *The
Collected Poems of Theodore Roethke*.
MACMILLAN, London and Basingstoke, for 'Picnic in Jammu'
from *Jets From Orange* by Zulfikar Ghose.
PHILIP M. SHERLOCK for 'Jamaican Fisherman' from *You
Better Believe It*.
EVAN JONES for 'The Lament of the Banana Man'.
OLIVE DEHN for 'The Park'.
NORTH WEST ARTS for 'Grandfather' by Susan Hrynkow
from *Young People's Poetry*, © 1970.
MRS PENELOPE MANDER for 'As It Was' from *Elegies*
by John Mander.
M.B. YEATS, MISS ANNE YEATS AND MACMILLAN, London
and Basingstoke, for 'The Fiddler of Dooney' from
Collected Poems by W.B. Yeats.

MAGIC AND MYSTERY

GEORGE ALLEN and UNWIN LTD. for 'Riddles', taken from
The Hobbit by J.R.R. Tolkien.
JENI COUZYN and the WORKSHOP PRESS LTD. for 'Warts'
(originally entitled 'The Soul is the Breath in your Body')
from *Flying*.
FABER AND FABER LTD. for 'O Where are you Going?' from
Collected Shorter Poems by W.H. Auden, and for 'Moon
Wind' from *Moon Bells and Other Poems* by Ted Hughes
(published by Chatto and Windus).
FABER AND FABER LTD. and ALFRED H. KNOPF, INC. for
'Ploughing on Sunday' from *The Collected Poems of
Wallace Stevens*.
MACMILLAN, London and Basingstoke, for 'The Discovery'
from *Collected Poems* by J.C. Squire.
ANGUS AND ROBERTSON (Sydney) for 'Full Moon Rhyme'
from *Collected Poems 1942-1970* by Judith Wright.
PENGUIN BOOKS LTD. for 'The Hare in the Moon' by
Ryōkan from *The Penguin Book of Japanese Verse*,
translated by Geoffrey Bownas and Anthony Thwaite
(Penguin Poets 1964).
TOM WRIGHT for ' High on the Hill'.
THE UNIVERSITY OF OKLAHOMA PRESS for 'Aztec Song' from
The Aztecs: People of the Sun by Alfonso Caso, translated
by Lowell Dunham, © 1958.
MRS A.M. WALSH for 'Is This All' (originally entitled
'Unhappy') from *The Roundabout by the Sea* by John
Walsh.
ROBERT GRAVES for 'Warning to Children' from *Collected
Poems*, © 1975.